Tower Vortx Digi Fryer Oven Cookbook UK 2024

1800 Days Healthy, Affordable and Fast Tower Air Fryer Recipes for Beginners with Tips & Tricks to Fry, Grill, Roast, and Bake

Shirley J. Simpson

All Rights Reserved.

The content contained within this book may not be reproduced, duplicated, or transmitted without direct written permission from the author or the publisher. Under no circumstances will any blame or legal responsibility be held against the publisher, or author, for any damages, reparation, or monetary loss due to the information contained within this book, either directly or indirectly.

Legal Notice: This book is copyright protected. It is only for personal use. You cannot amend, distribute, sell, use, quote or paraphrase any part, or the content within this book, without the consent of the author or publisher.

Disclaimer Notice:

Please note the information contained within this document is for educational and entertainment purposes only. All effort has been executed to present accurate, up to date, reliable, complete information. No warranties of any kind are declared or implied. Readers acknowledge that the author is not engaged in the rendering of legal, financial, medical, or professional advice. The content within this book has been derived from various sources. Please consult a licensed professional before attempting any techniques outlined in this book. By reading this document, the reader agrees that under no circumstances is the author responsible for any losses, direct or indirect, that are incurred as a result of the use of the information contained within this document, including, but not limited to, errors, omissions, or inaccuracies.

CONTENTS

MEASUREMENT CONVERSIONS 10

Breakfast & Snacks And Fries Recipes 12

Apple Crisps 12

Cheesy Sausage Breakfast Pockets 12

Muhammara 13

Easy Cheesy Scrambled Eggs 13

Healthy Stuffed Peppers 13

Wholegrain Pitta Chips 14

Breakfast Doughnuts 14

Avocado Fries 14

Meaty Egg Cups 15

Breakfast Sausage Burgers 15

Morning Sausage Wraps 15

Easy Cheese & Bacon Toasties 16

Baba Ganoush 16

Mexican Breakfast Burritos 17

Courgette Fries 17

Crunchy Mexican Breakfast Wrap 18

French Toast 18

Blueberry Bread 19

European Pancakes 19

Easy Air Fryer Sausage 19

Halloumi Fries 20

Bocconcini Balls 20

Raspberry Breakfast Pockets 20

Sauces & Snack And Appetiser Recipes 21

Pork Jerky 21

Popcorn Tofu 21

Corn Nuts 22

Peppers With Aioli Dip 22

Garlic Cheese Bread 22

3

Pepperoni Bread 23

Potato Patties 23

Italian Rice Balls 24

Garlic Pizza Toast 24

Thai Bites 25

Mozzarella Sticks 25

Snack Style Falafel 26

Jalapeño Pockets 26

Mac & Cheese Bites 27

Pretzel Bites 27

Korean Chicken Wings 28

Focaccia Bread 28

Waffle Fries 29

Lumpia 29

Roasted Almonds 29

Tasty Pumpkin Seeds 30

Beetroot Crisps 30

Vegetarian & Vegan Recipes 30

Saganaki 30

Spinach And Feta Croissants 31

Two-step Pizza 31

Quinoa-stuffed Romano Peppers 32

Aubergine Parmigiana 32

Butternut Squash Falafel 33

Artichoke Crostini 33

Bagel Pizza 34

Roast Cauliflower & Broccoli 34

Arancini 34

Artichoke Pasta 35

Spicy Spanish Potatoes 35

Crispy Potato Peels 35

Spring Ratatouille 36

Sweet Potato Taquitos 36

Tofu Bowls 37

Baked Feta, Tomato & Garlic Pasta 37

Bbq Soy Curls 38
Falafel Burgers 38
Air-fried Artichoke Hearts 39
Orange Zingy Cauliflower 39
Radish Hash Browns 40
Stuffed Peppers 40
Veggie Bakes 40
Rainbow Vegetables 41
Chickpea And Sweetcorn Falafel 41
Courgette Meatballs 42
Roasted Vegetable Pasta 42
Tempura Veggies 43
Mushroom Pasta 43
Spanakopita Bites 44
Sticky Tofu With Cauliflower Rice 44
Roasted Cauliflower 45
Veggie Lasagne 45

Beef & Lamb And Pork Recipes 46
Japanese Pork Chops 46
Char Siu Buffalo 46
Mongolian Beef 47
Roast Beef 47
Beef Wellington 47
Bbq Ribs 48
Vegetable & Beef Frittata 48
Beef Bulgogi Burgers 49
Traditional Empanadas 49
Steak Popcorn Bites 50
Cheeseburger Egg Rolls 50
Mustard Pork Tenderloin 51
Beef Nacho Pinwheels 51
Buttermilk Pork Chops 52
Crispy Chili Sausages 52
Sausage Gnocchi One Pot 52
Pork Chops With Raspberry And Balsamic 53

Sticky Asian Beef 53
Beef Stroganoff 54
Beef Stuffed Peppers 54
Kheema Meatloaf 55
Taco Lasagne Pie 55
Honey & Mustard Meatballs 56
Cheesy Beef Enchiladas 56
Pork Chops With Honey 56
Meatloaf 57
Parmesan Crusted Pork Chops 57
Lamb Burgers 58
Tahini Beef Bites 58
Tender Ham Steaks 58
Old Fashioned Steak 59
Pulled Pork, Bacon, And Cheese Sliders 59
Pork Taquitos 60
Chinese Pork With Pineapple 60

Fish & Seafood Recipes 61
Garlic-parsley Prawns 61
Shrimp Wrapped With Bacon 61
Garlic Tilapia 61
Traditional Fish And Chips 62
Copycat Fish Fingers 62
Tilapia Fillets 63
Cajun Prawn Skewers 63
Thai Salmon Patties 64
Cod In Parma Ham 64
Ranch Style Fish Fillets 65
Garlic Butter Salmon 65
Extra Crispy Popcorn Shrimp 65
Coconut Shrimp 66
Fish In Parchment Paper 66
Fish Sticks With Tartar Sauce Batter 67
Oat & Parmesan Crusted Fish Fillets 67
Salmon Patties 67

Air Fried Scallops	68
Store-cupboard Fishcakes	68
Honey Sriracha Salmon	68
Chilli Lime Tilapia	69
Mahi Fish Tacos	69
Cajun Shrimp Boil	70
Cod Nuggets	70

Poultry Recipes 71

Turkey And Mushroom Burgers	71
Hawaiian Chicken	71
Crunchy Chicken Tenders	72
Nashville Chicken	72
Chicken Jalfrezi	73
Healthy Bang Bang Chicken	73
Chicken Parmesan With Marinara Sauce	74
Satay Chicken Skewers	74
Chicken Fried Rice	75
Chicken Tikka Masala	75
Olive Stained Turkey Breast	76
Air Fried Maple Chicken Thighs	76
Pizza Chicken Nuggets	77
Honey Cajun Chicken Thighs	77
Chicken & Potatoes	78
Bacon Wrapped Chicken Thighs	78
Charred Chicken Breasts	79
Chicken Fajitas	79
Grain-free Chicken Katsu	80
Whole Chicken	81
Chicken And Cheese Chimichangas	81
Buffalo Chicken Wontons	81
Pepper & Lemon Chicken Wings	82

Side Dishes Recipes 82

Aubergine Parmesan	82
Hasselback New Potatoes	83

Butternut Squash Fries 83

Sweet Potato Tots 83

Onion Rings 84

Stuffed Jacket Potatoes 84

Ranch-style Potatoes 85

Asparagus Fries 85

Pumpkin Fries 85

Bbq Beetroot Crisps 86

Orange Sesame Cauliflower 86

Cheesy Garlic Asparagus 86

Crispy Broccoli 87

Grilled Bacon And Cheese 87

Asparagus Spears 87

Butternut Squash 88

Honey Roasted Parsnips 88

Super Easy Fries 88

Celery Root Fries 89

Shishito Peppers 89

Corn On The Cob 89

Sweet Potato Wedges 90

Yorkshire Puddings 90

Desserts Recipes 91

Pumpkin Spiced Bread Pudding 91

Profiteroles 91

Lemon Pies 92

Cinnamon-maple Pineapple Kebabs 92

Cherry Pies 92

Fruit Scones 93

Cinnamon Bites 93

Pop Tarts 94

Granola Bars 94

Sweet Potato Dessert Fries 95

Chocolate Eclairs 95

Blueberry Muffins 96

Banana Maple Flapjack 96

Oat-covered Banana Fritters 96

Zebra Cake 97

Banana Cake 97

Butter Cake 98

Birthday Cheesecake 98

S'mores 98

Chocolate Orange Muffins 99

Chocolate Soufflé 99

Pecan & Molasses Flapjack 100

Apple And Cinnamon Empanadas 100

Spiced Apples 100

Chocolate And Berry Pop Tarts 101

Chocolate Mug Cake 101

Christmas Biscuits 102

Strawberry Lemonade Pop Tarts 102

Chocolate-glazed Banana Slices 103

Crispy Snack Apples 103

Fruit Crumble 103

Pistachio Brownies 104

Grain-free Millionaire's Shortbread 104

RECIPES INDEX 105

MEASUREMENT CONVERSIONS

BASIC KITCHEN CONVERSIONS & EQUIVALENTS

DRY MEASUREMENTS CONVERSION CHART

3 TEASPOONS = 1 TABLESPOON = 1/16 CUP
6 TEASPOONS = 2 TABLESPOONS = 1/8 CUP
12 TEASPOONS = 4 TABLESPOONS = 1/4 CUP
24 TEASPOONS = 8 TABLESPOONS = 1/2 CUP
36 TEASPOONS = 12 TABLESPOONS = 3/4 CUP
48 TEASPOONS = 16 TABLESPOONS = 1 CUP

METRIC TO US COOKING CONVER-SIONS

OVEN TEMPERATURES

120 °C = 250 °F
160 °C = 320 °F
180 °C = 350 °F
205 °C = 400 °F
220 °C = 425 °F

LIQUID MEASUREMENTS CONVERSION CHART

8 FLUID OUNCES = 1 CUP = 1/2 PINT = 1/4 QUART
16 FLUID OUNCES = 2 CUPS = 1 PINT = 1/2 QUART
32 FLUID OUNCES = 4 CUPS = 2 PINTS = 1 QUART
1/4 GALLON
128 FLUID OUNCES = 16 CUPS = 8 PINTS = 4 QUARTS = 1 GALLON

BAKING IN GRAMS

1 CUP FLOUR = 140 GRAMS
1 CUP SUGAR = 150 GRAMS
1 CUP POWDERED SUGAR = 160 GRAMS
1 CUP HEAVY CREAM = 235 GRAMS

VOLUME

1 MILLILITER = 1/5 TEASPOON
5 ML = 1 TEASPOON
15 ML = 1 TABLESPOON
240 ML = 1 CUP OR 8 FLUID OUNCES
1 LITER = 34 FL. OUNCES

WEIGHT

1 GRAM = 035 OUNCES
100 GRAMS = 3.5 OUNCES
500 GRAMS = 1.1 POUNDS
1 KILOGRAM = 35 OUNCES

US TO METRIC COOKING CONVERSIONS

1/5 TSP = 1 ML
1 TSP = 5 ML
1 TBSP = 15 ML
1 FL OUNCE = 30 ML
1 CUP = 237 ML
1 PINT (2 CUPS) = 473 ML
1 QUART (4 CUPS) = .95 LITER
1 GALLON (16 CUPS) = 3.8 LITERS
1 OZ = 28 GRAMS
1 POUND = 454 GRAMS

BUTTER

1 CUP BUTTER = 2 STICKS = 8 OUNCES = 230 GRAMS = 8 TABLESPOONS

WHAT DOES 1 CUP EQUAL

1 CUP = 8 FLUID OUNCES
1 CUP = 16 TABLESPOONS
1 CUP = 48 TEASPOONS
1 CUP = 1/2 PINT
1 CUP = 1/4 QUART
1 CUP = 1/16 GALLON
1 CUP = 240 ML

BAKING PAN CONVERSIONS

1 CUP ALL-PURPOSE FLOUR = 4.5 OZ
1 CUP ROLLED OATS = 3 OZ 1 LARGE EGG = 1.7 OZ
1 CUP BUTTER = 8OZ 1 CUP MILK = 8 OZ
1 CUP HEAVY CREAM = 8.4 OZ
1 CUP GRANULATED SUGAR = 7.1 OZ
1 CUP PACKED BROWN SUGAR = 7.75 OZ
1 CUP VEGETABLE OIL = 7.7 OZ
1 CUP UNSIFTED POWDERED SUGAR = 4.4 OZ

BAKING PAN CONVERSIONS

9-INCH ROUND CAKE PAN = 12 CUPS
10-INCH TUBE PAN = 16 CUPS
11-INCH BUNDT PAN = 12 CUPS
9-INCH SPRINGFORM PAN = 10 CUPS
9 X 5 INCH LOAF PAN = 8 CUPS
9-INCH SQUARE PAN = 8 CUPS

Breakfast & Snacks And Fries Recipes

Apple Crisps

Servings: 2
Cooking Time:xx
Ingredients:
- 2 apples, chopped
- 1 tsp cinnamon
- 2 tbsp brown sugar
- 1 tsp lemon juice
- 2.5 tbsp plain flour
- 3 tbsp oats
- 2 tbsp cold butter
- Pinch of salt

Directions:
1. Preheat the air fryer to 260°C
2. Take a 5" baking dish and crease
3. Take a large bowl and combine the apples with the sugar, cinnamon and lemon juice
4. Add the mixture to the baking dish and cover with aluminium foil
5. Place in the air fryer and cook for 15 minutes
6. Open the lid and cook for another 5 minutes
7. Combine the rest of the ingredients in a food processor, until a crumble-type mixture occurs
8. Add over the top of the cooked apples
9. Cook with the lid open for another 5 minutes
10. Allow to cool a little before serving

Cheesy Sausage Breakfast Pockets

Servings: 2
Cooking Time:xx
Ingredients:
- 1 packet of regular puff pastry
- 4 sausages, cooked and crumbled into pieces
- 5 eggs
- 50g cooked bacon
- 50g grated cheddar cheese

Directions:
1. Scramble your eggs in your usual way
2. Add the sausage and the bacon as you are cooking the eggs and combine well
3. Take your pastry sheets and cut rectangular shapes
4. Add a little of the egg and meat mixture to one half of each pastry piece
5. Fold the rectangles over and use a fork to seal down the edges
6. Place your pockets into your air fryer and cook at 190°C for 10 minutes
7. Allow to cool before serving

Muhammara

Servings: 4
Cooking Time:xx

Ingredients:
- 4 romano peppers
- 4 tablespoons olive oil
- 100 g/1 cup walnuts
- 90 g/1 heaped cup dried breadcrumbs (see page 9)
- 1 teaspoon cumin
- 2 tablespoons pomegranate molasses
- freshly squeezed juice of ½ a lemon
- ½ teaspoon chilli/chili salt (or salt and some chilli/hot red pepper flakes combined)
- fresh pomegranate seeds, to serve

Directions:
1. Preheat the air-fryer to 180°C/350°F.
2. Rub the peppers with ½ teaspoon of the olive oil. Add the peppers to the preheated air-fryer and air-fry for 8 minutes.
3. Meanwhile, lightly toast the walnuts by tossing them in a shallow pan over a medium heat for 3–5 minutes. Allow to cool, then grind the walnuts in a food processor. Once the peppers are cooked, chop off the tops and discard most of the seeds. Add to the food processor with all other ingredients. Process until smooth. Allow to cool in the fridge, then serve the dip with pomegranate seeds on top.

Easy Cheesy Scrambled Eggs

Servings: 1
Cooking Time:xx

Ingredients:
- 1 tbsp butter
- 2 eggs
- 100g grated cheese
- 2 tbsp milk
- Salt and pepper for seasoning

Directions:
1. Add the butter inside the air fryer pan and cook at 220°C until the butter has melted
2. Add the eggs and milk to a bowl and combine, seasoning to your liking
3. Pour the eggs into the butter panned cook for 3 minutes, stirring around lightly to scramble
4. Add the cheese and cook for another 2 more minutes

Healthy Stuffed Peppers

Servings: 2
Cooking Time:xx

Ingredients:
- 1 large bell pepper, deseeded and cut into halves
- 1 tsp olive oil
- 4 large eggs
- Salt and pepper to taste

Directions:
1. Take your peppers and rub a little olive oil on the edges
2. Into each pepper, crack one egg and season with salt and pepper
3. You will need to insert a trivet into your air fryer to hold the peppers, and then arrange the peppers evenly
4. Set your fryer to 200°C and cook for 13 minutes
5. Once cooked, remove and serve with a little more seasoning, if required

Wholegrain Pitta Chips

Servings: 2
Cooking Time:xx
Ingredients:
- 2 round wholegrain pittas, chopped into quarters
- 1 teaspoon olive oil
- ½ teaspoon garlic salt

Directions:
1. Preheat the air-fryer to 180°C/350°F.
2. Spray or brush each pitta quarter with olive oil and sprinkle with garlic salt. Place in the preheated air-fryer and air-fry for 4 minutes, turning halfway through cooking. Serve immediately.

Breakfast Doughnuts

Servings: 4
Cooking Time:xx
Ingredients:
- 1 packet of Pillsbury Grands
- 5 tbsp raspberry jam
- 1 tbsp melted butter
- 5 tbsp sugar

Directions:
1. Preheat your air fryer to 250°C
2. Place the Pillsbury Grands into the air fryer and cook for around 5m minutes
3. Remove and place to one side
4. Take a large bowl and add the sugar
5. Coat the doughnuts in the melted butter, coating evenly
6. Dip into the sugar and coat evenly once more
7. Using an icing bag, add the jam into the bag and pipe an even amount into each doughnut
8. Eat warm or cold

Avocado Fries

Servings: 2
Cooking Time:xx
Ingredients:
- 35 g/¼ cup plain/all-purpose flour (gluten free if you wish)
- ½ teaspoon chilli/chili powder
- 1 egg, beaten
- 50 g/heaped ½ cup dried breadcrumbs (gluten-free if you wish; see page 9)
- 1 avocado, skin and stone removed, and each half sliced lengthways
- salt and freshly ground black pepper

Directions:
1. Preheat the air-fryer to 200°C/400°F.
2. In a bowl combine the flour and chilli/chili powder, then season with salt and pepper. Place the beaten egg in a second bowl and the breadcrumbs in a third bowl.
3. Dip each avocado slice in the seasoned flour (shaking off any excess), then the egg and finally the breadcrumbs.
4. Add the breaded avocado slices to the preheated air-fryer and air-fry for 6 minutes, turning after 4 minutes. Serve immediately.

Meaty Egg Cups

Servings: 4
Cooking Time:xx
Ingredients:
- 8 slices of toasted sandwich bread
- 2 slices of ham
- 4 eggs
- Salt and pepper to taste
- Butter for greasing

Directions:
1. Take 4 ramekins and grease the insides with a little butter
2. Flatten the slices of toast with a rolling pin and arrange inside the ramekins - two in each
3. Line the inside of each ramekin with a slice of ham
4. Crack one egg into each ramekin
5. Season with a little salt and pepper
6. Place the ramekins into the air fryer and cook at 160°C for 15 minutes
7. Remove from the fryer and wait to cool just slightly
8. Remove and serve

Breakfast Sausage Burgers

Servings: 2
Cooking Time:xx
Ingredients:
- 8 links of your favourite sausage
- Salt and pepper to taste

Directions:
1. Remove the sausage from the skins and use a fork to create a smooth mixture
2. Season to your liking
3. Shape the sausage mixture into burgers or patties
4. Preheat your air fryer to 260°C
5. Arrange the burgers in the fryer, so they are not touching each other
6. Cook for 8 minutes
7. Serve still warm

Morning Sausage Wraps

Servings: 8
Cooking Time:xx
Ingredients:
- 8 sausages, chopped into pieces
- 2 slices of cheddar cheese, cut into quarters
- 1 can of regular crescent roll dough
- 8 wooden skewers

Directions:
1. Take the dough and separate each one
2. Cut open the sausages evenly
3. The one of your crescent rolls and on the widest part, add a little sausage and then a little cheese
4. Roll the dough and tuck it until you form a triangle
5. Repeat this for four times and add into your air fryer
6. Cook at 190°C for 3 minutes
7. Remove your dough and add a skewer for serving
8. Repeat with the other four pieces of dough

Easy Cheese & Bacon Toasties

Servings: 2
Cooking Time:xx

Ingredients:
- 4 slices of sandwich bread
- 2 slices of cheddar cheese
- 5 slices of pre-cooked bacon
- 1 tbsp melted butter
- 2 slices of mozzarella cheese

Directions:
1. Take the bread and spread the butter onto one side of each slice
2. Place one slice of bread into the fryer basket, buttered side facing downwards
3. Place the cheddar on top, followed by the bacon, mozzarella and the other slice of bread on top, buttered side upwards
4. Set your fryer to 170ºC
5. Cook for 4 minutes and then turn over and cook for another 3 minutes
6. Serve whilst still hot

Baba Ganoush

Servings: 4
Cooking Time:xx

Ingredients:
- 1 large aubergine/eggplant, sliced in half lengthways
- ½ teaspoon salt
- 5 tablespoons olive oil
- 1 bulb garlic
- 30 g/2 tablespoons tahini or nut butter
- 2 tablespoons freshly squeezed lemon juice
- ½ teaspoon ground cumin
- ¼ teaspoon smoked paprika
- salt and freshly ground black pepper
- 3 tablespoons freshly chopped flat-leaf parsley

Directions:
1. Preheat the air-fryer to 200ºC/400ºF.
2. Lay the aubergine/eggplant halves cut side up. Sprinkle over the salt, then drizzle over 1 tablespoon of oil. Cut the top off the garlic bulb, brush the exposed cloves with a little olive oil, then wrap in foil. Place the aubergine/eggplant and foil-wrapped garlic in the preheated air-fryer and air-fry for 15–20 minutes until the inside of the aubergine is soft and buttery in texture.
3. Scoop the flesh of the aubergine into a bowl. Squeeze out about 1 tablespoon of the cooked garlic and add to the bowl with the remaining 4 tablespoons of olive oil, the tahini/nut butter, lemon juice, spices and salt and pepper to taste. Mix well and serve with fresh flat-leaf parsley sprinkled over.

Mexican Breakfast Burritos

Servings: 6
Cooking Time:xx

Ingredients:
- 6 scrambled eggs
- 6 medium tortillas
- Half a minced red pepper
- 8 sausages, cut into cubes and browned
- 4 pieces of bacon, pre-cooked and cut into pieces
- 65g grated cheese of your choice
- A small amount of olive oil for cooking

Directions:
1. Into a regular mixing bowl, combine the eggs, bell pepper, bacon pieces, the cheese, and the browned sausage, giving everything a good stir
2. Take your first tortilla and place half a cup of the mixture into the middle, folding up the top and bottom and rolling closed
3. Repeat until all your tortillas have been used
4. Arrange the burritos into the bottom of your fryer and spray with a little oil
5. Cook the burritos at 170°C for 5 minutes

Courgette Fries

Servings: 2
Cooking Time:xx

Ingredients:
- 1 courgette/zucchini
- 3 tablespoons plain/all-purpose flour (gluten-free if you wish)
- ¼ teaspoon salt
- ¼ teaspoon freshly ground black pepper
- 60 g/¾ cup dried breadcrumbs (gluten-free if you wish; see page 9)
- 1 teaspoon dried oregano
- 20 g/¼ cup finely grated Parmesan
- 1 egg, beaten

Directions:
1. Preheat the air-fryer to 180°C/350°F.
2. Slice the courgette/zucchini into fries about 1.5 x 1.5 x 5 cm/⅝ x ⅝ x 2 in.
3. Season the flour with salt and pepper. Combine the breadcrumbs with the oregano and Parmesan.
4. Dip the courgettes/zucchini in the flour (shaking off any excess flour), then the egg, then the seasoned breadcrumbs.
5. Add the fries to the preheated air-fryer and air-fry for 15 minutes. They should be crispy on the outside but soft on the inside. Serve immediately.

Crunchy Mexican Breakfast Wrap

Servings: 2
Cooking Time:xx
Ingredients:
- 2 large tortillas
- 2 corn tortillas
- 1 sliced jalapeño pepper
- 4 tbsp ranchero sauce
- 1 sliced avocado
- 25g cooked pinto beans

Directions:
1. Take each of your large tortillas and add the egg, jalapeño, sauce, the corn tortillas, the avocado and the pinto beans, in that order. If you want to add more sauce at this point, you can
2. Fold over your wrap to make sure that nothing escapes
3. Place each wrap into your fryer and cook at 190°C for 6 minutes
4. Remove your wraps and place in the oven, cooking for a further 5 minutes at 180°C, until crispy
5. Place each wrap into a frying pan and crisp a little more on a low heat, for a couple of minutes on each side

French Toast

Servings: 2
Cooking Time:xx
Ingredients:
- 2 beaten eggs
- 2 tbsp softened butter
- 4 slices of sandwich bread
- 1 tsp cinnamon
- 1 tsp nutmeg
- 1 tsp ground cloves
- 1 tsp maple syrup

Directions:
1. Preheat your fryer to 180°C
2. Take a bowl and add the eggs, salt, cinnamon, nutmeg, and cloves, combining well
3. Take your bread and butter each side, cutting into strips
4. Dip the bread slices into the egg mixture
5. Arrange each slice into the basket of your fryer
6. Cook for 2 minutes
7. Take the basket out and spray with a little cooking spray
8. Turn over the slices and place back into the fryer
9. Cook for 4 minutes
10. Remove and serve with maple syrup

Blueberry Bread

Servings: 8
Cooking Time:xx
Ingredients:
- 260ml milk
- 3 eggs
- 25g protein powder
- 400g frozen blueberries
- 600g bisquick or pancake mixture

Directions:
1. Take a large mixing bowl and combine all ingredients until smooth
2. Preheat the air fryer to 250°C
3. Place the mixture into a loaf tin
4. Place the tin into the air fryer and cook for 30 minutes
5. A toothpick should come out clean if the bread is cooked

European Pancakes

Servings: 5
Cooking Time:xx
Ingredients:
- 3 large eggs
- 130g flour
- 140ml whole milk
- 2 tbsp unsweetened apple sauce
- A pinch of salt

Directions:
1. Set your fryer to 200°C and add five ramekins inside to heat up
2. Place all your ingredients inside a blender to combine
3. Spray the ramekins with a little cooking spray
4. Pour the batter into the ramekins carefully
5. Fry for between 6-8 minutes, depending on your preference
6. Serve with your favourite toppings

Easy Air Fryer Sausage

Servings: 5
Cooking Time:xx
Ingredients:
- 5 uncooked sausages
- 1 tbsp mustard
- Salt and pepper for seasoning

Directions:
1. Line the basket of your fryer with parchment paper
2. Arrange the sausages inside the basket
3. Set to 180°C and cook for 15 minutes
4. Turn the sausages over and cook for another 5 minutes
5. Remove and cool
6. Drizzle the mustard over the top and season to your liking

Halloumi Fries

Servings: 2
Cooking Time:xx
Ingredients:
- 225 g/8 oz. halloumi
- 40 g/heaped ¼ cup plain/all-purpose flour (gluten-free if you wish)
- ½ teaspoon sweet smoked paprika
- ½ teaspoon dried oregano
- ¼ teaspoon mild chilli/chili powder
- olive oil or avocado oil, for spraying

Directions:
1. Preheat the air-fryer to 180°C/350°F.
2. Slice the halloumi into fries roughly 2 x 1.5 cm/¾ x ⅝ in.
3. Mix the flour and seasoning in a bowl and dip each halloumi stick into the flour to coat. Spray with a little oil.
4. Add the fries to the preheated air-fryer and air-fry for 5 minutes. Serve immediately.

Bocconcini Balls

Servings: 2
Cooking Time:xx
Ingredients:
- 70 g/½ cup plus ½ tablespoon plain/all-purpose flour (gluten-free if you wish)
- 1 egg, beaten
- 70 g/1 cup dried breadcrumbs (gluten-free if you wish; see page 9)
- 10 bocconcini

Directions:
1. Preheat the air-fryer to 200°C/400°F.
2. Place the flour, egg and breadcrumbs on 3 separate plates. Dip each bocconcini ball first in the flour to coat, then the egg, shaking off any excess before rolling in the breadcrumbs.
3. Add the breaded bocconcini to the preheated air-fryer and air-fry for 5 minutes (no need to turn them during cooking). Serve immediately.

Raspberry Breakfast Pockets

Servings: 1
Cooking Time:xx
Ingredients:
- 2 slices of sandwich bread
- 1 tbsp soft cream cheese
- 1 tbsp raspberry jam
- 1 tbsp milk
- 1 egg

Directions:
1. Take one slice of the bread and add one tablespoon of jam into the middle
2. Take the second slice and add the cream cheese into the middle
3. Using a blunt knife, spread the jam and the cheese across the bread, but don't go to the outer edges
4. Take a small bowl and whisk the eggs and the milk together
5. Set your fryer to 190°C and spray with a little oil
6. Dip your sandwich into the egg and arrange inside your fryer
7. Cook for 5 minutes on the first side, turn and cook for another 2 minutes

Sauces & Snack And Appetiser Recipes

Pork Jerky

Servings: 35
Cooking Time:xx
Ingredients:
- 300g mince pork
- 1 tbsp oil
- 1 tbsp sriracha
- 1 tbsp soy
- ½ tsp pink curing salt
- 1 tbsp rice vinegar
- ½ tsp salt
- ½ tsp pepper
- ½ tsp onion powder

Directions:
1. Mix all ingredients in a bowl until combined
2. Refrigerate for about 8 hours
3. Shape into sticks and place in the air fryer
4. Heat the air fryer to 160°C
5. Cook for 1 hour turn then cook for another hour
6. Turn again and cook for another hour
7. Cover with paper and sit for 8 hours

Popcorn Tofu

Servings: 4
Cooking Time:xx
Ingredients:
- 400g firm tofu
- 100g chickpea flour
- 100g oatmeal
- 2 tbsp yeast
- 150ml milk
- 400g breadcrumbs
- 1 tsp garlic powder
- 1 tsp onion powder
- 1 tbsp dijon mustard
- ½ tsp salt
- ½ tsp pepper
- 2 tbsp vegetable bouillon

Directions:
1. Rip the tofu into pieces. Place the breadcrumbs into a bowl, in another bowl mix the remaining ingredients
2. Dip the tofu into the batter mix and then dip into the breadcrumbs
3. Heat the air fryer to 175°C
4. Place the tofu in the air fryer and cook for 12 minutes shaking halfway through

Corn Nuts
Servings: 8
Cooking Time:xx
Ingredients:
- 1 giant white corn
- 3 tbsp vegetable oil
- 2 tsp salt

Directions:
1. Place the corn in a large bowl, cover with water and sit for 8 hours
2. Drain, pat dry and air dry for 20 minutes
3. Preheat the air fryer to 200°C
4. Place in a bowl and coat with oil and salt
5. Cook in the air fryer for 10 minutes shake then cook for a further 10 minutes

Peppers With Aioli Dip
Servings: 4
Cooking Time:xx
Ingredients:
- 250g shishito peppers
- 2 tsp avocado oil
- 5 tbsp mayonnaise
- 2 tbsp lemon juice
- 1 minced clove of garlic
- 1 tbsp chopped parsley
- Salt and pepper for seasoning

Directions:
1. Take a medium bowl and combine the mayonnaise with the lemon juice, garlic, parsley and seasoning and create a smooth dip
2. Preheat the air fryer to 220°C
3. Toss the peppers in the oil and add to the air fryer
4. Cook for 4 minutes, until the peppers are soft and blistered on the outside
5. Remove and serve with the dip

Garlic Cheese Bread
Servings: 2
Cooking Time:xx
Ingredients:
- 250g grated mozzarella
- 50g grated parmesan
- 1 egg
- ½ tsp garlic powder

Directions:
1. Line air fryer with parchment paper
2. Mix ingredients in a bowl
3. Press into a circle onto the parchment paper in the air fryer
4. Heat the air fryer to 175°C
5. Cook for 10 minutes

Pepperoni Bread

Servings: 4
Cooking Time:xx

Ingredients:
- Cooking spray
- 400g pizza dough
- 200g pepperoni
- 1 tbsp dried oregano
- Ground pepper to taste
- Garlic salt to taste
- 1 tsp melted butter
- 1 tsp grated parmesan
- 50g grated mozzarella

Directions:
1. Line a baking tin with 2 inch sides with foil to fit in the air fryer
2. Spray with cooking spray
3. Preheat the air fryer to 200°C
4. Roll the pizza dough into 1 inch balls and line the baking tin
5. Sprinkle with pepperoni, oregano, pepper and garlic salt
6. Brush with melted butter and sprinkle with parmesan
7. Place in the air fryer and cook for 15 minutes
8. Sprinkle with mozzarella and cook for another 2 minutes

Potato Patties

Servings: 12
Cooking Time:xx

Ingredients:
- 150g instant mash
- 50g peas and carrots
- 2 tbsp coriander
- 1 tbsp oil
- 100ml hot water
- ½ tsp turmeric
- ½ tsp cayenne
- ½ tsp salt
- ½ tsp cumin seeds
- ¼ tsp ground cumin

Directions:
1. Place all the ingredients in a bowl. Mix well cover and stand for 10 minutes
2. Preheat the air fryer to 200°C
3. Spray the air fryer with cooking spray
4. Make 12 patties, place in the air fryer and cook for 10 minutes

Italian Rice Balls

Servings: 2
Cooking Time:xx

Ingredients:
- 400g cooked rice
- 25g breadcrumbs, plus an extra 200g for breading
- 2 tbsp flour, plus an extra 2 tbsp for breading
- 1 tbsp cornstarch, plus an extra 3 tbsp for breading
- 1 chopped bell pepper
- 1 chopped onion
- 2 tbsp olive oil
- 1 tsp red chilli flakes
- 5 chopped mozzarella cheese sticks
- A little water for the breading
- Salt and pepper for seasoning

Directions:
1. Place the cooked rice into a bowl and mash with a fork. Place to one side
2. Take a saucepan and add the oil, salting the onion and peppers until they're both soft
3. Add the chilli flakes and a little salt and combine
4. Add the mixture to the mashed rice and combine
5. Add the 2 tbsp flour and 1 tbsp cornstarch, along with the 25g breadcrumbs and combine well
6. Use your hands to create balls with the mixture
7. Stuff a piece of the mozzarella inside the balls and form around it
8. Take a bowl and add the rest of the flour, corn starch and a little seasoning, with a small amount of water to create a thick batter
9. Take another bowl and add the rest of the breadcrumbs
10. Dip each rice ball into the batter and then the breadcrumbs
11. Preheat the air fryer to 220°C
12. Cook for 6 minutes, before shaking and cooking for another 6 minutes

Garlic Pizza Toast

Servings: 8
Cooking Time:xx

Ingredients:
- 1 pack garlic Texas toast, or 8 slices of bread topped with garlic butter
- 100g pizza sauce
- 50g pepperoni
- 100g grated cheese

Directions:
1. Top each piece of toast with pizza sauce
2. Add cheese and pepperoni
3. Heat air fryer to 190°C
4. Place in the air fryer and cook for 5 minutes

Thai Bites

Servings: 4
Cooking Time:xx

Ingredients:
- 400g pork mince
- 1 onion
- 1 tsp garlic paste
- 1 tbsp soy
- 1 tbsp Worcester sauce
- Salt and pepper
- 2 tsp Thai curry paste
- ½ lime juice and zest
- 1 tsp mixed spice
- 1 tsp Chinese spice
- 1 tsp coriander

Directions:
1. Place all ingredients in a bowl and mix well
2. Shape into balls
3. Place in the air fryer and cook at 180°C for 15 minutes

Mozzarella Sticks

Servings: 4
Cooking Time:xx

Ingredients:
- 60ml water
- 50g flour
- 5 tbsp cornstarch
- 1 tbsp cornmeal
- 1 tsp garlic powder
- ½ tsp salt
- 100g breadcrumbs
- ½ tsp pepper
- ½ tsp parsley
- ½ tsp onion powder
- ¼ tsp oregano
- ½ tsp basil
- 200g mozzarella cut into ½ inch strips

Directions:
1. Mix water, flour, cornstarch, cornmeal, garlic powder and salt in a bowl
2. Stir breadcrumbs, pepper, parsley, onion powder, oregano and basil together in another bowl
3. Dip the mozzarella sticks in the batter then coat in the breadcrumbs
4. Heat the air fryer to 200°C
5. Cook for 6 minutes turn and cook for another 6 minutes

Snack Style Falafel

Servings: 15
Cooking Time:xx

Ingredients:
- 150g dry garbanzo beans
- 300g coriander
- 75g flat leaf parsley
- 1 red onion, quartered
- 1 clove garlic
- 2 tbsp chickpea flour
- Cooking spray
- 1 tbsp cumin
- 1 tbsp coriander
- 1 tbsp sriracha
- ½ tsp baking powder
- Salt and pepper to taste
- ¼ tsp baking soda

Directions:
1. Add all ingredients apart from the baking soda and baking powder to a food processor and blend well
2. Cover and rest for 1 hour
3. Heat air fryer to 190ºC
4. Add baking powder and baking soda to mix and combine
5. Form mix into 15 equal balls
6. Spray air fryer with cooking spray
7. Add to air fryer and cook for 8-10 minutes

Jalapeño Pockets

Servings: 4
Cooking Time:xx

Ingredients:
- 1 chopped onion
- 60g cream cheese
- 1 jalapeño, chopped
- 8 wonton wrappers
- ¼ tsp garlic powder
- ⅛ tsp onion powder

Directions:
1. Cook the onion in a pan for 5 minutes until softened
2. Add to a bowl and mix with the remaining ingredients
3. Lay the wonton wrappers out and add filling to each one
4. Fold over to create a triangle and seal with water around the edges
5. Heat the air fryer to 200ºC
6. Place in the air fryer and cook for about 4 minutes

Mac & Cheese Bites

Servings: 14
Cooking Time:xx
Ingredients:
- 200g mac and cheese
- 2 eggs
- 200g panko breadcrumbs
- Cooking spray

Directions:
1. Place drops of mac and cheese on parchment paper and freeze for 1 hour
2. Beat the eggs in a bowl, add the breadcrumbs to another bowl
3. Dip the mac and cheese balls in the egg then into the breadcrumbs
4. Heat the air fryer to 190°C
5. Place in the air fryer, spray with cooking spray and cook for 15 minutes

Pretzel Bites

Servings: 2
Cooking Time:xx
Ingredients:
- 650g flour
- 2.5 tsp active dry yeast
- 260ml hot water
- 1 tsp salt
- 4 tbsp melted butter
- 2 tbsp sugar

Directions:
1. Take a large bowl and add the flour, sugar and salt
2. Take another bowl and combine the hot water and yeast, stirring until the yeast has dissolved
3. Then, add the yeast mixture to the flour mixture and use your hands to combine
4. Knead for 2 minutes
5. Cover the bowl with a kitchen towel for around half an hour
6. Divide the dough into 6 pieces
7. Preheat the air fryer to 260°C
8. Take each section of dough and tear off a piece, rolling it in your hands to create a rope shape, that is around 1" in thickness
9. Cut into 2" strips
10. Place the small dough balls into the air fryer and leave a little space in-between
11. Cook for 6 minutes
12. Once cooked, remove and brush with melted butter and sprinkle salt on top

Korean Chicken Wings

Servings: 2
Cooking Time:xx

Ingredients:
- 25ml soy sauce
- 40g brown sugar
- 2 tbsp hot pepper paste
- 1 tsp sesame oil
- ½ tsp ginger paste
- ½ tsp garlic paste
- 2 green onions, chopped
- 400g chicken wings
- 1 tbsp vegetable oil

Directions:
1. Preheat air fryer to 200°C
2. Place all ingredients apart from chicken wings and vegetable oil in a pan and simmer for about 4 minutes set aside
3. Massage the vegetable oil into the chicken wings
4. Place in the air fryer and cook for about 10 minutes
5. Turn and cook for a further 10 minutes
6. Coat the wings in the sauce and return to the air fryer
7. Cook for about 2 minutes

Focaccia Bread

Servings: 8
Cooking Time:xx

Ingredients:
- 500g pizza dough
- 3 tbsp olive oil
- 2-3 garlic cloves, chopped
- ¼ tsp red pepper flakes
- 50g parsley
- 1 tsp basil
- 100g chopped red peppers
- 60g black olives halved
- 60g green olives halved
- Salt and pepper to taste

Directions:
1. Preheat the air fryer to 180°C, make indentations in the pizza dough with your finger tips and set aside
2. Heat the olive oil in a pan add the garlic and cook for a few minutes, add the remaining ingredients and cook for another 5-8 minutes not letting the oil get too hot
3. Spread the oil mix over the dough with a spatula
4. Place in the air fryer and cook for 12-15 minutes

Waffle Fries

Servings: 4
Cooking Time:xx
Ingredients:
- 2 large potatoes, russet potatoes work best
- 1 tsp salt for seasoning
- Waffle cutter

Directions:
1. Peel the potatoes and slice using the waffle cutter. You can also use a mandolin cutter that has a blade
2. Transfer the potatoes to a bowl and season with the salt, coating evenly
3. Add to the air fryer and cook at 220°C for 15 minutes, shaking every so often

Lumpia

Servings: 16
Cooking Time:xx
Ingredients:
- 400g Italian sausage
- 1 sliced onion
- 1 chopped carrot
- 50g chopped water chestnuts
- Cooking spray
- 2 cloves minced, garlic
- 2 tbsp soy sauce
- ½ tsp salt
- ¼ tsp ground ginger
- 16 spring roll wrappers

Directions:
1. Cook sausage in a pan for about 5 minutes. Add green onions, onions, water chestnuts and carrot cook for 7 minutes
2. Add garlic and cook for a further 2 minutes
3. Add the soy sauce, salt and ginger, stir to mix well
4. Add filling to each spring roll wrapper.
5. Roll over the bottom and tuck in the sides, continue to roll up the spring roll
6. Spray with cooking spray and place in the air fryer
7. Cook at 200°C for 4 minutes turn and cook for a further 4 minutes

Roasted Almonds

Servings: 2
Cooking Time:xx
Ingredients:
- 1 tbsp soy sauce
- 1 tbsp garlic powder
- 1 tsp paprika
- ¼ tsp pepper
- 400g raw almonds

Directions:
1. Place all of the ingredients apart from the almonds in a bowl and mix
2. Add the almonds and coat well
3. Place the almonds in the air fryer and cook at 160°C for 6 minutes shaking every 2 minutes

Tasty Pumpkin Seeds

Servings: 2
Cooking Time:xx
Ingredients:
- 1 ¾ cups pumpkin seeds
- 2 tsp avocado oil
- 1 tsp paprika
- 1 tsp salt

Directions:
1. Preheat air fryer to 180°C
2. Add all ingredients to a bowl and mix well
3. Place in the air fryer and cook for 35 minutes shaking frequently

Beetroot Crisps

Servings: 2
Cooking Time:xx
Ingredients:
- 3 medium beetroots
- 2 tbsp oil
- Salt to taste

Directions:
1. Peel and thinly slice the beetroot
2. Coat with the oil and season with salt
3. Preheat the air fryer to 200°C
4. Place in the air fryer and cook for 12-18 minutes until crispy

Vegetarian & Vegan Recipes

Saganaki

Servings: 2
Cooking Time:xx
Ingredients:
- 200 g/7 oz. kefalotyri or manouri cheese, sliced into wedges 1 cm/½ in. thick
- 2 tablespoons plain/all-purpose flour
- olive oil, for drizzling

Directions:
1. Preheat the air-fryer to 200°C/400°F.
2. Dip each wedge of cheese in the flour, then tap off any excess. Drizzle olive oil onto both sides of the cheese slices
3. Add the cheese to the preheated air-fryer and air-fry for 3 minutes. Remove from the air-fryer and serve.

Spinach And Feta Croissants

Servings: 4
Cooking Time: 10 Minutes

Ingredients:
- 4 pre-made croissants
- 100 g / 7 oz feta cheese, crumbled
- 1 tsp dried chives
- 1 tsp garlic powder
- 50 g / 3.5 oz fresh spinach, chopped

Directions:
1. Preheat the air fryer to 180 °C / 350 °F. Remove the mesh basket from the air fryer machine and line with parchment paper.
2. Cut the croissants in half and lay each half out on the lined mesh basket.
3. In a bowl, combine the crumbled feta cheese, dried chives, garlic powder, and chopped spinach until they form a consistent mixture.
4. Spoon some of the mixture one half of the four croissants and cover with the second half of the croissants to seal in the filling.
5. Carefully slide the croissants in the mesh basket into the air fryer machine, close the lid, and cook for 10 minutes until the pastry is crispy and the feta cheese has melted.

Two-step Pizza

Servings: 1
Cooking Time: xx

Ingredients:
- BASE
- 130 g/generous ½ cup Greek yogurt
- 125 g self-raising/self-rising flour, plus extra for dusting
- ¼ teaspoon salt
- PIZZA SAUCE
- 100 g/3½ oz. passata/strained tomatoes
- 1 teaspoon dried oregano
- ¼ teaspoon garlic salt
- TOPPINGS
- 75 g/2½ oz. mozzarella, torn
- fresh basil leaves, to garnish

Directions:
1. Mix together the base ingredients in a bowl. Once the mixture starts to look crumbly, use your hands to bring the dough together into a ball. Transfer to a piece of floured parchment paper and roll to about 5 mm/¼ in. thick. Transfer to a second piece of non-floured parchment paper.
2. Preheat the air-fryer to 200°C/400°F.
3. Meanwhile, mix the pizza sauce ingredients together in a small bowl and set aside.
4. Prick the pizza base all over with a fork and transfer (on the parchment paper) to the preheated air-fryer and air-fry for 5 minutes. Turn the pizza base over and top with the pizza sauce and the torn mozzarella. Cook for a further 3–4 minutes, until the cheese has melted. Serve immediately with the basil scattered over the top.

Quinoa-stuffed Romano Peppers

Servings: 2
Cooking Time:xx

Ingredients:
- 1 tablespoon olive oil
- 1 onion, diced
- 1 garlic clove, chopped
- 100 g/⅔ cup uncooked quinoa
- 1½ tablespoons fajita seasoning
- 140 g/1 cup canned sweetcorn/corn kernels (drained weight)
- 3 romano peppers, sliced lengthways, seeds removed but stalk left intact
- 60 g/⅔ cup grated mature Cheddar

Directions:
1. Heat the oil in a saucepan. Add the onion and garlic and sauté for 5 minutes, until soft. Add the quinoa, fajita seasoning and 250 ml/1 cup water. Bring to a simmer, then cover with a lid and simmer for 15 minutes or until the quinoa is cooked and the water absorbed. Stir in the sweetcorn/corn kernels. Stuff each pepper half with the quinoa mixture, then top with grated cheese.
2. Preheat the air-fryer to 180°C/350°F.
3. Place the peppers on an air-fryer liner or a piece of pierced parchment paper, place in the preheated air-fryer and air-fry for 12–14 minutes, depending how 'chargrilled' you like your peppers.

Aubergine Parmigiana

Servings: 2 As A Main Or 4 As A Side
Cooking Time:xx

Ingredients:
- 2 small or 1 large aubergine/eggplant, sliced 5 mm/¼ in. thick
- 1 tablespoon olive oil
- ¾ teaspoon salt
- 200 g/7 oz. mozzarella, sliced
- ½ teaspoon freshly ground black pepper
- 20 g/¼ cup finely grated Parmesan
- green vegetables, to serve
- SAUCE
- 135 g/5 oz. passata/strained tomatoes
- 1 teaspoon dried oregano
- ¼ teaspoon garlic salt
- 1 tablespoon olive oil

Directions:
1. Preheat the air-fryer to 200°C/400°F.
2. Rub each of the aubergine/eggplant slices with olive oil and salt. Divide the slices into two batches. Place one batch of the aubergine slices in the preheated air-fryer and air-fry for 4 minutes on one side, then turn over and air-fry for 2 minutes on the other side. Lay these on the base of a gratin dish that fits into your air-fryer.
3. Air-fry the second batch of aubergine slices in the same way. Whilst they're cooking, mix together the sauce ingredients in a small bowl.
4. Spread the sauce over the aubergines in the gratin dish. Add a layer of the mozzarella slices, then season with pepper. Add a second layer of aubergine slices, then top with Parmesan.
5. Place the gratin dish in the air-fryer and air-fry for 6 minutes, until the mozzarella is melted and the top of the dish is golden brown. Serve immediately with green vegetables on the side.

Butternut Squash Falafel

Servings: 2
Cooking Time:xx

Ingredients:
- 500 g/1 lb. 2 oz. frozen butternut squash cubes
- 1 tablespoon olive oil, plus extra for cooking
- 100 g/¾ cup canned or cooked chickpeas (drained weight)
- 20 g/¼ cup gram/chickpea flour
- 1 teaspoon ground cumin
- ½ teaspoon ground coriander
- ½ teaspoon salt

Directions:
1. Preheat the air-fryer to 180°C/350°F.
2. Toss the frozen butternut squash in the olive oil. Add to the preheated air-fryer and air-fry for 12–14 minutes, until soft but not caramelized. Remove from the air-fryer and mash the squash by hand or using a food processor, then combine with the chickpeas, flour, spices and salt. Leave the mixture to cool, then divide into 6 equal portions and mould into patties.
3. Preheat the air-fryer to 180°C/350°F.
4. Spray the patties with a little olive oil, then add to the preheated air-fryer and air-fry for 10 minutes, turning once (carefully) during cooking. Enjoy hot or cold.

Artichoke Crostini

Servings: 2
Cooking Time:xx

Ingredients:
- 100g cashews
- 1 tbsp olive oil
- 1 tbsp lemon juice
- 1 tsp balsamic vinegar
- 3 tbsp hummus
- 200g grilled artichoke hearts
- ½ tsp basil
- ½ tsp oregano
- ⅛ tsp onion powder
- 1 clove garlic minced
- Salt
- 1 baguette cut in ½ inch slices

Directions:
1. Combine cashews, olive oil, lemon juice, balsamic vinegar, basil oregano, onion powder, garlic and salt in a bowl. Set aside
2. Place the baguette slices in the air fryer and cook at 180°C for 3-4 minutes
3. Sprinkle the baguette slices with cashew mix then add the artichoke hearts
4. Serve with hummus

Bagel Pizza

Servings: 1
Cooking Time:xx

Ingredients:
- 1 bagel
- 2 tbsp marinara sauce
- 6 slices vegan pepperoni
- 2 tbsp mozzarella
- Pinch of basil

Directions:
1. Heat the air fryer to 180°C
2. Cut the bagel in half and toast for 2 minutes in the air fryer
3. Remove from the air fryer and top with marinara sauce, pepperoni and mozzarella
4. Return to the air fryer and cook for 4-5 minutes
5. Sprinkle with basil to serve

Roast Cauliflower & Broccoli

Servings: 6
Cooking Time:xx

Ingredients:
- 300g broccoli
- 300g cauliflower
- 2 tbsp oil
- ½ tsp garlic powder
- ¼ tsp salt
- ¼ tsp paprika
- ⅛ tsp pepper

Directions:
1. Preheat air fryer to 200°C
2. Place broccoli and cauliflower in a bowl and microwave for 3 minutes
3. Add remaining ingredients and mix well
4. Add to the air fryer and cook for about 12 mins

Arancini

Servings: 12
Cooking Time:xx

Ingredients:
- 1 batch of risotto
- 100g panko breadcrumbs
- 1 tsp onion powder
- Salt and pepper
- 300ml warm marinara sauce

Directions:
1. Take ¼ cup risotto and form a rice ball
2. Mix the panko crumbs, onion powder, salt and pepper
3. Coat the risotto ball in the crumb mix
4. Place in the air fryer, spray with oil and cook at 200°C for 10 minutes
5. Serve with marinara sauce

Artichoke Pasta

Servings: 2
Cooking Time:xx

Ingredients:
- 100g pasta
- 50g basil leaves
- 6 artichoke hearts
- 2 tbsp pumpkin seeds
- 2 tbsp lemon juice
- 1 clove garlic
- ½ tsp white miso paste
- 1 can chickpeas
- 1 tsp olive oil

Directions:
1. Place the chickpeas in the air fryer and cook at 200°C for 12 minutes
2. Cook the pasta according to packet instructions
3. Add the remaining ingredients to a food processor and blend
4. Add the pasta to a bowl and spoon over the pesto mix
5. Serve and top with roasted chickpeas

Spicy Spanish Potatoes

Servings: 2
Cooking Time:xx

Ingredients:
- 4 large potatoes
- 1 tbsp olive oil
- 2 tsp paprika
- 2 tsp dried garlic
- 1 tsp barbacoa seasoning
- Salt and pepper

Directions:
1. Chop the potatoes into wedges
2. Place them in a bowl with olive oil and seasoning, mix well
3. Add to the air fryer and cook at 160°C for 20 minutes
4. Shake, increase heat to 200°C and cook for another 3 minutes

Crispy Potato Peels

Servings: 1
Cooking Time:xx

Ingredients:
- Peels from 4 potatoes
- Cooking spray
- Salt to season

Directions:
1. Heat the air fryer to 200°C
2. Place the peels in the air fryer spray with oil and sprinkle with salt
3. Cook for about 6-8 minutes until crispy

Spring Ratatouille

Servings:2
Cooking Time:15 Minutes

Ingredients:
- 1 tbsp olive oil
- 4 Roma tomatoes, sliced
- 2 cloves garlic, minced
- 1 courgette, cut into chunks
- 1 red pepper and 1 yellow pepper, cut into chunks
- 2 tbsp mixed herbs
- 1 tbsp vinegar

Directions:
1. Preheat the air fryer to 190 °C / 370 °F and line the air fryer with parchment paper or grease it with olive oil.
2. Place all of the ingredients into a large mixing bowl and mix until fully combined.
3. Transfer the vegetables into the lined air fryer basket, close the lid, and cook for 15 minutes until the vegetables have softened.

Sweet Potato Taquitos

Servings: 10
Cooking Time:xx

Ingredients:
- 1 sweet potato cut into ½ inch pieces
- 1 ½ tsp oil
- 1 chopped onion
- 1 tsp minced garlic
- 400g black beans
- 3 tbsp water
- 10 corn tortillas
- 1 chipotle pepper, chopped
- ½ tsp cumin
- ½ tsp paprika
- ½ chilli powder
- ⅛ tsp salt
- ½ tsp maple syrup

Directions:
1. Place the sweet potato in the air fryer spray with oil and cook for 12 minutes at 200°C
2. Heat oil in a pan, add the onion and garlic and cook for a few minutes until soft
3. Add remaining ingredients to the pan, add 2 tbsp of water and combine
4. Add the sweet potato and 1 tbsp of water and mix
5. Warm the tortilla in the microwave for about 1 minute
6. Place a row of filling across the centre of each tortilla. Fold up the bottom of the tortilla, tuck under the filling, fold in the edges then continue to roll the tortilla
7. Place in the air fryer and cook for about 12 minutes

Tofu Bowls

Servings: 4
Cooking Time:xx
Ingredients:
- 1 block of tofu, cut into cubes
- 40ml soy sauce
- 2 tbsp sesame oil
- 1 tsp garlic powder
- 1 chopped onion
- 2 tbsp Tahini dressing
- 3 bunches baby bok choy, chopped
- 300g quinoa
- 1 medium cucumber, sliced
- 1 cup shredded carrot
- 1 avocado, sliced

Directions:
1. Mix the soy sauce, 1 tbsp sesame oil and garlic powder in a bowl. Add the tofu marinade for 10 minutes
2. Place in the air fryer and cook at 200°C for 20 minutes turning halfway
3. Heat the remaining sesame oil in a pan and cook the onions for about 4 minutes
4. Add the bok choy and cook for another 4 minutes
5. Divide the quinoa between your bowls add bok choy, carrot, cucumber and avocado. Top with the tofu and drizzle with Tahini

Baked Feta, Tomato & Garlic Pasta

Servings: 2
Cooking Time:xx
Ingredients:
- 100 g/3½ oz. feta or plant-based feta, cubed
- 20 cherry tomatoes
- 2 garlic cloves, peeled and halved
- ¾ teaspoon oregano
- 1 teaspoon chilli/hot red pepper flakes
- ½ teaspoon garlic salt
- 2 tablespoons olive oil
- 100 g/3½ oz. cooked pasta plus about 1 tablespoon of cooking water
- freshly ground black pepper

Directions:
1. Preheat the air-fryer to 200°C/400°F.
2. Place the feta, tomatoes and garlic in a baking dish that fits inside your air-fryer. Top with the oregano, chilli/hot red pepper flakes, garlic salt and olive oil. Place the dish in the preheated air-fryer and air-fry for 10 minutes, then remove and stir in the pasta and cooking water. Serve sprinkled with black pepper.

Bbq Soy Curls

Servings: 2
Cooking Time:xx
Ingredients:
- 250ml warm water
- 1 tsp vegetable bouillon
- 200g soy curls
- 40g BBQ sauce
- 1 tsp oil

Directions:
1. Soak the soy curls in water and bouillon for 10 minutes
2. Place the soy curls in another bowl and shred
3. Heat the air fryer to 200°C
4. Cook for 3 minutes
5. Remove from the air fryer and coat in bbq sauce
6. Return to the air fryer and cook for 5 minutes shaking halfway through

Falafel Burgers

Servings: 2
Cooking Time:xx
Ingredients:
- 1 large can of chickpeas
- 1 onion
- 1 lemon
- 140g oats
- 28g grated cheese
- 28g feta cheese
- Salt and pepper to taste
- 3 tbsp Greek yogurt
- 4 tbsp soft cheese
- 1 tbsp garlic puree
- 1 tbsp coriander
- 1 tbsp oregano
- 1 tbsp parsley

Directions:
1. Place the chickpeas, onion, lemon rind, garlic and seasonings and blend until coarse
2. Add the mix to a bowl and stir in half the soft cheese, cheese and feta
3. Form in to burger shape and coat in the oats
4. Place in the air fryer and cook at 180°C for 8 minutes
5. To make the sauce mix the remaining soft cheese, greek yogurt and lemon juice in a bowl

Air-fried Artichoke Hearts

Servings: 7
Cooking Time:xx
Ingredients:
- 14 artichoke hearts
- 200g flour
- ¼ tsp baking powder
- Salt
- 6 tbsp water
- 6 tbsp breadcrumbs
- ¼ tsp basil
- ¼ tsp oregano
- ¼ tsp garlic powder
- ¼ tsp paprika

Directions:
1. Mix the baking powder, salt, flour and water in a bowl
2. In another bowl combine the breadcrumbs and seasonings
3. Dip the artichoke in the batter then coat in breadcrumbs
4. Place in the air fryer and cook at 180°C for 8 minutes

Orange Zingy Cauliflower

Servings: 2
Cooking Time:xx
Ingredients:
- 200ml water
- 200g flour
- Half the head of a cauliflower, cut into 1.5" florets
- 2 tsp olive oil
- 2 minced garlic cloves
- 1 tsp minced ginger
- 150ml orange juice
- 3 tbsp white vinegar
- 1/2 tsp red pepper flakes
- 1 tsp sesame oil 100g brown sugar
- 3 tbsp soy sauce
- 1 tbsp cornstarch
- 2 tbsp water
- 1 tsp salt

Directions:
1. Take a medium mixing bowl and add the water, salt and flour together
2. Dip each floret of cauliflower into the mixture and place in the air fryer basket
3. Cook at 220°C for 15 minutes
4. Meanwhile make the orange sauce by combining all ingredients in a saucepan and allowing to simmer for 3 minutes, until the sauce has thickened
5. Drizzle the sauce over the cauliflower to serve

Radish Hash Browns

Servings: 4
Cooking Time:xx
Ingredients:
- 300g radish
- 1 onion
- 1 tsp onion powder
- ¾ tsp sea salt
- ½ tsp paprika
- ¼ tsp ground black pepper
- 1 tsp coconut oil

Directions:
1. Wash the radish, trim off the roots and slice in a processor along with the onions
2. Add the coconut oil and mix well
3. Put the onions and radish into the air fryer and cook at 180°C for 8 minutes shaking a few times
4. Put the onion and radish in a bowl add seasoning and mix well
5. Put back in the air fryer and cook at 200°C for 5 minutes

Stuffed Peppers

Servings: 6
Cooking Time:xx
Ingredients:
- 250g diced potatoes
- 100g peas
- 1 small onion, diced
- 1 carrot, diced
- 1 bread roll, diced
- 2 garlic cloves, minced
- 2 tsp mixed herbs
- 6 bell peppers
- 100g grated cheese

Directions:
1. Preheat air fryer to 180°C
2. Combine all the ingredients together apart from the peppers
3. Stuff the peppers with the mix
4. Place in the air fryer and cook for about 20 minutes

Veggie Bakes

Servings: 2
Cooking Time:xx
Ingredients:
- Any type of leftover vegetable bake you have
- 30g flour

Directions:
1. Preheat the air fryer to 180°C
2. Mix the flour with the leftover vegetable bake
3. Shape into balls and place in the air fryer
4. Cook for 10 minutes

Rainbow Vegetables

Servings: 4
Cooking Time:xx
Ingredients:
- 1 red pepper, cut into slices
- 1 squash sliced
- 1 courgette sliced
- 1 tbsp olive oil
- 150g sliced mushrooms
- 1 onion sliced
- Salt and pepper to taste

Directions:
1. Preheat air fryer to 180°C
2. Place all ingredients in a bowl and mix well
3. Place in the air fryer and cook for about 20 minutes turning halfway

Chickpea And Sweetcorn Falafel

Servings:4
Cooking Time:15 Minutes
Ingredients:
- ½ onion, sliced
- 2 cloves garlic, peeled and sliced
- 2 tbsp fresh parsley, chopped
- 2 tbsp fresh coriander, chopped
- 2 x 400 g / 14 oz chickpeas, drained and rinsed
- 1 tsp salt
- 1 tsp black pepper
- 1 tsp baking powder
- 1 tsp dried mixed herbs
- 1 tsp cumin
- 1 tsp chili powder
- 50 g / 1.8 oz sweetcorn, fresh or frozen

Directions:
1. Preheat the air fryer to 180 °C / 350 °F and line the bottom of the basket with parchment paper.
2. In a food processor, place the onion, garlic cloves, fresh parsley, and fresh coriander. Pulse the ingredients in 30-second intervals until they form a smooth mixture. Scrape the mixture from the sides of the food processor in between each interval if necessary.
3. Mix in the chickpeas, salt, black pepper, baking powder, dried mixed herbs, cumin, and chili powder. Pulse the mixture until fully combined and smooth. Add more water if the mixture is looking a bit dry. The mixture should be dry but not crumbly.
4. Use a spoon to scoop out 2 tbsp of the chickpea mixture at a time and roll into small, even falafels.
5. Transfer the falafels into the prepared air fryer basket and cook for 12-15 minutes.
6. Serve the falafels either hot or cold as a side dish to your main meal or as part of a large salad.

Courgette Meatballs

Servings: 4
Cooking Time: xx
Ingredients:
- 400g oats
- 40g feta, crumbled
- 1 beaten egg
- Salt and pepper
- 150g courgette
- 1 tsp lemon rind
- 6 basil leaves, thinly sliced
- 1 tsp dill
- 1 tsp oregano

Directions:
1. Preheat the air fryer to 200°C
2. Grate the courgette into a bowl, squeeze any access water out
3. Add all the remaining ingredients apart from the oats and mix well
4. Blend the oats until they resemble breadcrumbs
5. Add the oats into the other mix and stir well
6. Form into balls and place in the air fryer cook for 10 minutes

Roasted Vegetable Pasta

Servings: 4
Cooking Time: 15 Minutes
Ingredients:
- 400 g / 14 oz penne pasta
- 1 courgette, sliced
- 1 red pepper, deseeded and sliced
- 100 g / 3.5 oz mushroom, sliced
- 2 tbsp olive oil
- 1 tsp Italian seasoning
- 200 g cherry tomatoes, halved
- 2 tbsp fresh basil, chopped
- ½ tsp black pepper

Directions:
1. Cook the pasta according to the packet instructions.
2. Preheat the air fryer to 190 °C / 370 °F and line the air fryer with parchment paper or grease it with olive oil.
3. In a bowl, place the courgette, pepper, and mushroom, and toss in 2 tbsp olive oil
4. Place the vegetables in the air fryer and cook for 15 minutes.
5. Once the vegetables have softened, mix with the penne pasta, chopped cherry tomatoes, and fresh basil.
6. Serve while hot with a sprinkle of black pepper in each dish.

Tempura Veggies

Servings: 4
Cooking Time:xx

Ingredients:
- 150g flour
- ½ tsp salt
- ½ tsp pepper
- 2 eggs
- 2 tbsp cup water
- 100g avocado wedges
- 100g courgette slices
- 100g panko breadcrumbs
- 2 tsp oil
- 100g green beans
- 100g asparagus spears
- 100g red onion rings
- 100g pepper rings

Directions:
1. Mix together flour, salt and pepper. In another bowl mix eggs and water
2. Stir together panko crumbs and oil in a separate bowl
3. Dip vegetables in the flour mix, then egg and then the bread crumbs
4. Preheat the air fryer to 200°C
5. Place in the air fryer and cook for about 10 minutes until golden brown

Mushroom Pasta

Servings: 4
Cooking Time:xx

Ingredients:
- 250g sliced mushrooms
- 1 chopped onion
- 2 tsp minced garlic
- 1 tsp salt
- ½ tsp red pepper flakes
- 75g cup cream
- 70g mascarpone
- 1 tsp dried thyme
- 1 tsp ground black pepper
- ½ cup grated parmesan

Directions:
1. Place all the ingredients in a bowl and mix well
2. Heat the air fryer to 175°C
3. Grease a 7x3 inch pan and pour in the mixture
4. Place in the air fryer and cook for 15 minutes stirring halfway through
5. Pour over cooked pasta and sprinkle with parmesan

Spanakopita Bites

Servings: 4
Cooking Time:xx
Ingredients:
- 300g baby spinach
- 2 tbsp water
- 100g cottage cheese
- 50g feta cheese
- 2 tbsp grated parmesan
- 1 tbsp olive oil
- 4 sheets of filo pastry
- 1 large egg white
- 1 tsp lemon zest
- 1 tsp oregano
- ¼ tsp salt
- ¼ tsp pepper
- ⅛ tsp cayenne

Directions:
1. Place spinach in water and cook for about 5 minutes, drain
2. Mix all ingredients together
3. Place a sheet of pastry down and brush with oil, place another on the top and do the same, continue until all four on top of each other
4. Ut the pastry into 8 strips then cut each strip in half across the middle
5. Add 1 tbsp of mix to each piece of pastry
6. Fold one corner over the mix to create a triangle, fold over the other corner to seal
7. Place in the air fryer and cook at 190°C for about 12 minutes until golden brown

Sticky Tofu With Cauliflower Rice

Servings:4
Cooking Time:20 Minutes
Ingredients:
- For the tofu:
- 1 x 180 g / 6 oz block firm tofu
- 2 tbsp soy sauce
- 1 onion, sliced
- 1 large carrot, peeled and thinly sliced
- For the cauliflower:
- 200 g / 7 oz cauliflower florets
- 2 tbsp soy sauce
- 1 tbsp sesame oil
- 2 cloves garlic, minced
- 100 g / 3.5 oz broccoli, chopped into small florets

Directions:
1. Preheat the air fryer to 190 °C / 370 °F and line the air fryer with parchment paper or grease it with olive oil.
2. Crumble the tofu into a bowl and mix in the soy sauce, and the sliced onion and carrot.
3. Cook the tofu and vegetables in the air fryer for 10 minutes.
4. Meanwhile, place the cauliflower florets into a blender and pulse until it forms a rice-like consistency.
5. Place the cauliflower rice in a bowl and mix in the soy sauce, sesame oil, minced garlic cloves, and broccoli florets until well combined. Transfer to the air fryer and cook for 10 minutes until hot and crispy.

Roasted Cauliflower

Servings: 2
Cooking Time:xx
Ingredients:
- 3 cloves garlic
- 1 tbsp peanut oil
- ½ tsp salt
- ½ tsp paprika
- 400g cauliflower florets

Directions:
1. Preheat air fryer to 200°C
2. Crush the garlic, place all ingredients in a bowl and mix well
3. Place in the air fryer and cook for about 15 minutes, shaking every 5 minutes

Veggie Lasagne

Servings: 1
Cooking Time:xx
Ingredients:
- 2 lasagne sheets
- Pinch of salt
- 100g pasta sauce
- 50g ricotta
- 60g chopped basil
- 40g chopped spinach
- 3 tbsp grated courgette

Directions:
1. Break the lasagne sheets in half, bring a pan of water to boil
2. Cook the lasagne sheets for about 8 minutes, drain and pat dry
3. Add 2 tbsp of pasta sauce to a mini loaf tin
4. Add a lasagne sheet, top with ricotta, basil and spinach, then add courgette
5. Place another lasagne sheet on top
6. Add a couple of tbsp pasta sauce, basil, spinach and courgette
7. Add the last lasagne sheet, top with pasta sauce and ricotta
8. Cover with foil and place in the air fryer
9. Cook at 180°C for 10 mins, remove foil and cook for another 3 minutes

Beef & Lamb And Pork Recipes

Japanese Pork Chops

Servings: 4
Cooking Time:xx
Ingredients:
- 6 boneless pork chops
- 30g flour
- 2 beaten eggs
- 2 tbsp sweet chilli sauce
- 500g cup seasoned breadcrumbs
- ⅛ tsp salt
- ⅛ tsp pepper
- Tonkatsu sauce to taste

Directions:
1. Place the flour, breadcrumbs and eggs in 3 separate bowls
2. Sprinkle both sides of the pork with salt and pepper
3. Coat the pork in flour, egg and then breadcrumbs
4. Place in the air fryer and cook at 180°C for 8 minutes, turn then cook for a further 5 minutes
5. Serve with sauces on the side

Char Siu Buffalo

Servings: 2
Cooking Time:xx
Ingredients:
- 1 kg beef, cut into strips
- 4 tbsp honey
- 2 tbsp sugar
- 2 tbsp char siu sauce
- 2 tbsp oyster sauce
- 2 tbsp soy sauce
- 2 tbsp olive oil
- 2 tsp minced garlic
- ¼ tsp bi carbonate of soda

Directions:
1. Place all the ingredients in a bowl, mix well and marinate over night
2. Line the air fryer with foil, add the beef, keep the marinade to one side
3. Cook at 200°C for 10 minutes
4. Brush the pork with the sauce and cook for another 20 minutes at 160°C
5. Remove the meat and set aside
6. Strain the marinade into a saucepan, heat until it thickens
7. Drizzle over the pork and serve with rice

Mongolian Beef

Servings: 4
Cooking Time:xx

Ingredients:
- 500g steak
- 25g cornstarch
- 2 tsp vegetable oil
- ½ tsp ginger
- 1 tbsp garlic minced
- 75g soy sauce
- 75g water
- 100g brown sugar

Directions:
1. Slice the steak and coat in corn starch
2. Place in the air fryer and cook at 200°C for 10 minutes turning halfway
3. Place remaining ingredients in a sauce pan and gently warm
4. When cooked place the steak in a bowl and pour the sauce over

Roast Beef

Servings: 2
Cooking Time:xx

Ingredients:
- 400g beef fillet
- 1 tbsp olive oil
- 1 tsp salt
- 1 tsp rosemary

Directions:
1. Preheat the air fryer to 180°C
2. Mix salt, rosemary and oil on a plate
3. Coat the beef with the mix
4. Place the beef in the air fryer and cook for 45 minutes turning halfway

Beef Wellington

Servings: 4
Cooking Time:xx

Ingredients:
- 300g chicken liver pate
- 500g shortcrust pastry
- 600g beef fillet
- 1 egg beaten
- Salt and pepper

Directions:
1. Remove all the visible fat from the beef season with salt and pepper. Wrap in cling film and place in the fridge for 1 hour
2. Roll out the pastry, brush the edges with egg
3. Spread the pate over the pastry. Remove the clingfilm from the beef and place in the center of the pastry
4. Seal the pastry around the meat
5. Place in the air fryer and cook at 160°C for 35 minutes

Bbq Ribs

Servings: 2
Cooking Time:xx

Ingredients:
- 500g ribs
- 3 chopped garlic cloves
- 4 tbsp bbq sauce
- 1 tbsp honey
- ½ tsp five spice
- 1 tsp sesame oil
- 1 tsp salt
- 1 tsp black pepper
- 1 tsp soy sauce

Directions:
1. Chop the ribs into small pieces and place them in a bowl
2. Add all the ingredients into the bowl and mix well
3. Marinate for 4 hours
4. Preheat the air fryer to 180°C
5. Place the ribs into the air fryer and cook for 15 minutes
6. Coat the ribs in honey and cook for a further 15 minutes

Vegetable & Beef Frittata

Servings: 2
Cooking Time:xx

Ingredients:
- 250g ground beef
- 4 shredded hash browns
- 8 eggs
- Half a diced onion
- 1 courgette, diced
- 250g grated cheese
- Salt and pepper for seasoning

Directions:
1. Break the ground beef up and place in the air fryer
2. Add the onion and combine well
3. Cook at 260°C for 3 minutes
4. Stir the mixture and cook foremother 2 minutes
5. Remove and clean the tray
6. Add the courgette to the air fryer and spray with a little cooking oil
7. Cook for 3 minutes
8. Add to the meat mixture and combine
9. Take a mixing bowl and combine the cheese, has browns, and eggs
10. Add the meat and courgette to the bowl and season with salt and pepper
11. Take a 6" round baking tray and add the mixture
12. Cook for 8 minutes before cutting lines in the top and cooking for another 8 minutes
13. Cut into slices before serving

Beef Bulgogi Burgers

Servings: 4
Cooking Time:xx
Ingredients:
- 500g minced beef
- 2 tbsp gochujang
- 1 tbsp soy
- 2 tsp minced garlic
- 2 tsp minced ginger
- 2 tsp sugar
- 1 tbsp olive oil
- 1 chopped onion

Directions:
1. Mix all the ingredients in a large bowl, allow to rest for at least 30 minutes in the fridge
2. Divide the meat into four and form into patties
3. Place in the air fryer and cook at 180°C for about 10 minutes
4. Serve in burger buns, if desired

Traditional Empanadas

Servings: 2
Cooking Time:xx
Ingredients:
- 300g minced beef
- 1 tbsp olive oil
- ¼ cup finely chopped onion
- 150g chopped mushrooms
- ⅛ tsp cinnamon
- 4 chopped tomatoes
- 2 tsp chopped garlic
- 6 green olives
- ¼ tsp paprika
- ¼ tsp cumin
- 8 goyoza wrappers
- 1 beaten egg

Directions:
1. Heat oil in a pan add onion and minced beef and cook until browned
2. Add mushrooms and cook for 6 minutes
3. Add garlic, olives, paprika, cumin and cinnamon, and cook for about 3 minutes
4. Stir in tomatoes and cook for 1 minute, set aside allow to cool
5. Place 1 ½ tbsp of filling in each goyoza wrapper
6. Brush edges with egg fold over and seal pinching edges
7. Place in the air fryer and cook at 200 for about 7 minutes

Steak Popcorn Bites

Servings: 4
Cooking Time:xx

Ingredients:

- 500g steak, cut into 1" sized cubes
- 500g potato chips, ridged ones work best
- 100g flour
- 2 beaten eggs
- Salt and pepper to taste

Directions:

1. Place the chips into the food processor and pulse unit you get fine chip crumbs
2. Take a bowl and combine the flour with salt and pepper
3. Add the chips to another bowl and the beaten egg to another bowl
4. Take the steak cubes and dip first in the flour, then the egg and then the chip crumbs
5. Preheat your air fryer to 260°C
6. Place the steak pieces into the fryer and cook for 9 minutes

Cheeseburger Egg Rolls

Servings: 4
Cooking Time:xx

Ingredients:

- 400g minced beef
- ¼ tsp garlic powder
- ¼ tsp onion powder
- 1 chopped red pepper
- 1 chopped onion
- 6 dill pickles, chopped
- Salt and pepper
- 3 tbsp grated cheese
- 3 tbsp cream cheese
- 2 tbsp ketchup
- 1 tbsp mustard
- 6 large egg roll wrappers

Directions:

1. Cook the pepper, onion and minced beef in a pan for about 5 minutes
2. Remove from heat and stir in cheese, cream cheese, ketchup and mustard
3. Put the mix into a bowl and stir in the pickles
4. Place ⅙ of the mix in the centre of each wrap, moisten the edges with water roll up the wrap around the mixture and seal
5. Set your fryer to 200°C and cook for about 7 minutes
6. Turn the sandwich over and cook for another 3 minutes
7. Turn the sandwich out and serve whilst hot
8. Repeat with the other remaining sandwich

Mustard Pork Tenderloin

Servings: 2
Cooking Time:xx

Ingredients:
- 1 pork tenderloin
- 3 tbsp soy sauce
- 2 minced garlic cloves
- 3 tbsp olive oil
- 2 tbsp brown sugar
- 1 tbsp dijon mustard
- Salt and pepper for seasoning

Directions:
1. Take a bowl and combine the ingredients, except for the pork
2. Pour the mixture into a ziplock bag and then add the pork
3. Close the top and make sure the pork is well covered
4. Place in the refrigerator for 30minutes
5. Preheat your air fryer to 260°C
6. Remove the pork from the bag and place in the fryer
7. Cook for 25 minutes, turning halfway
8. Remove and rest for 5 minutes before slicing into pieces

Beef Nacho Pinwheels

Servings: 6
Cooking Time:xx

Ingredients:
- 500g minced beef
- 1 packet of taco seasoning
- 300ml water
- 300ml sour cream
- 6 tostadas
- 6 flour tortillas
- 3 tomatoes
- 250g nacho cheese
- 250g shredded lettuce
- 250g Mexican cheese

Directions:
1. Preheat air fryer to 200°C
2. Brown the mince in a pan and add the taco seasoning
3. Share the remaining ingredients between the tortillas
4. Fold the edges of the tortillas up towards the centre, should look like a pinwheel
5. Lay seam down in the air fryer and cook for 2 minutes
6. Turnover and cook for a further 2 minutes

Buttermilk Pork Chops

Servings: 4
Cooking Time:xx
Ingredients:
- 4 pork chops
- 3 tbsp buttermilk
- 75g flour
- Cooking oil spray
- 1 packet of pork rub
- Salt and pepper to taste

Directions:
1. Rub the chops with the pork rub
2. Place the pork chops in a bowl and drizzle with buttermilk
3. Coat the chops with flour
4. Place in the air fryer and cook at 190°C for 15 minutes turning halfway

Crispy Chili Sausages

Servings:4
Cooking Time:20 Minutes
Ingredients:
- 8 sausages, uncooked
- 2 eggs
- ½ tsp salt
- ½ black pepper
- ½ tsp chili flakes
- ½ tsp paprika

Directions:
1. Preheat the air fryer to 180 °C / 350 °F and line the bottom of the basket with parchment paper.
2. Place the sausages in the air fryer and cook for 5 minutes until slightly browned, but not fully cooked. Remove from the air fryer and set aside.
3. While the sausages are cooking, whisk together the eggs, salt, black pepper, chili flakes, and paprika. Coat the sausages evenly in the egg and spice mixture.
4. Return the sausages to the air fryer and cook for a further 5 minutes until brown and crispy.
5. Eat the sausages while hot with a side of steamed vegetables or place them in a sandwich for lunch.

Sausage Gnocchi One Pot

Servings: 2
Cooking Time:xx
Ingredients:
- 4 links of sausage
- 250g green beans, washed and cut into halves
- 1 tsp Italian seasoning
- 1 tbsp olive oil
- 300g gnocchi
- Salt and pepper for seasoning

Directions:
1. Preheat the air fryer to 220°C
2. Cut the sausage up into pieces
3. Take a bowl and add the gnocchi and green beans, along with the oil and season
4. Place the sausage into the fryer first and then the rest of the ingredients
5. Cook for 12 minutes, giving everything a stir halfway through

Pork Chops With Raspberry And Balsamic

Servings: 4
Cooking Time:xx
Ingredients:
- 2 large eggs
- 30ml milk
- 250g panko bread crumbs
- 250g finely chopped pecans
- 1 tbsp orange juice
- 4 pork chops
- 30ml balsamic vinegar
- 2 tbsp brown sugar
- 2 tbsp raspberry jam

Directions:
1. Preheat air fryer to 200°C
2. Mix the eggs and milk together in a bowl
3. In another bowl mix the breadcrumbs and pecans
4. Coat the pork chops in flour, egg and then coat in the breadcrumbs
5. Place in the air fryer and cook for 12 minutes until golden turning halfway
6. Put the remaining ingredients in a pan simmer for about 6 minutes, serve with the pork chops

Sticky Asian Beef

Servings: 2
Cooking Time:xx
Ingredients:
- 1 tbsp coconut oil
- 2 sliced peppers
- 25g liquid aminos
- 25g cup water
- 100g brown sugar
- ¼ tsp pepper
- ½ tsp ground ginger
- ½ tbsp minced garlic
- 1 tsp red pepper flakes
- 600g steak thinly sliced
- ¼ tsp salt

Directions:
1. Melt the coconut oil in a pan, add the peppers and cook until softened
2. In another pan add the aminos, brown sugar, ginger, garlic and pepper flakes. Mix and bring to the boil, simmer for 10 mins
3. Season the steak with salt and pepper
4. Put the steak in the air fryer and cook at 200°C for 10 minutes. Turn the steak and cook for a further 5 minutes until crispy
5. Add the steak to the peppers then mix with the sauce
6. Serve with rice

Beef Stroganoff

Servings: 4
Cooking Time: 20 Minutes
Ingredients:
- 4 cubes / 800 ml beef stock cubes
- 4 tbsp olive oil
- 1 onion, chopped
- 200 g / 7 oz sour cream
- 200 g / 7 oz mushroom, finely sliced
- 500 g / 17.6 oz steak, chopped
- 4 x 100 g / 3.5 oz egg noodles, cooked

Directions:
1. Preheat the air fryer to 200 °C / 400 °F and line the bottom of the basket with parchment paper.
2. Boil 800 ml of water and use it to dissolve the 4 beef stock cubes.
3. In a heat-proof bowl, mix the olive oil, onion, sour cream, mushrooms, and beef stock until fully combined.
4. Coat all sides of the steak chunks in the mixture and set aside to marinate for 10 minutes.
5. Transfer the steak to the air fryer, close the lid, and cook for 10 minutes. Serve the steak hot with a serving of egg noodles.

Beef Stuffed Peppers

Servings: 4
Cooking Time: xx
Ingredients:
- 4 bell peppers
- ½ chopped onion
- 1 minced garlic clove
- 500g minced beef
- 5 tbsp tomato sauce
- 100g grated cheese
- 2 tsp Worcestershire sauce
- 1 tsp garlic powder
- A pinch of black pepper
- ½ tsp chilli powder
- 1 tsp dried basil
- 75g cooked rice

Directions:
1. Cook the onions, minced beef, garlic and all the seasonings until the meat is browned
2. Remove from the heat and add Worcestershire sauce, rice, ½ the cheese and ⅔ of the tomato sauce mix well
3. Cut the tops off the peppers and remove the seeds
4. Stuff the peppers with the mixture and place in the air fryer
5. Cook at 200°C for about 11 minutes
6. When there are 3 minutes remaining top the peppers with the rest of the tomato sauce and cheese

Kheema Meatloaf

Servings: 4
Cooking Time:xx

Ingredients:
- 500g minced beef
- 2 eggs
- 1 diced onion
- 200g sliced coriander
- 1 tbsp minced ginger
- ⅛ cardamom pod
- 1 tbsp minced garlic
- 2 tsp garam masala
- 1 tsp salt
- 1 tsp cayenne
- 1 tsp turmeric
- ½ tsp cinnamon

Directions:
1. Place all the ingredients in a large bowl and mix well
2. Place meat in an 8 inch pan and set air fryer to 180°C
3. Place in the air fryer and cook for 15 minutes
4. Slice and serve

Taco Lasagne Pie

Servings: 4
Cooking Time:xx

Ingredients:
- 450g ground beef
- 2 tbsp olive oil
- 1 chopped onion
- 1 minced garlic clove
- 1 tsp cumin
- 1 tsp oregano
- 1/2 tsp adobo
- 266g grated Cheddar cheese
- 4 flour tortillas
- 112g tomato sauce

Directions:
1. Soften the onions with the olive oil in a frying pan
2. Add the beef and garlic until the meat has browned
3. Add the tomato sauce, cumin, oregano, and adobo and combine
4. Allow to simmer for a few minutes
5. Place one tortilla on the bottom of your air fryer basket
6. Add a meat layer, followed by a layer of the cheese, and continue alternating this routine until you have no meat left
7. Add a tortilla on top and sprinkle with the rest of the cheese
8. Cook at 180°C for 8 minutes

Honey & Mustard Meatballs

Servings: 4
Cooking Time:xx
Ingredients:
- 500g minced pork
- 1 red onion
- 1 tsp mustard
- 2 tsp honey
- 1 tsp garlic puree
- 1 tsp pork seasoning
- Salt and pepper

Directions:
1. Thinly slice the onion
2. Place all the ingredients in a bowl and mix until well combined
3. Form into meatballs, place in the air fryer and cook at 180°C for 10 minutes

Cheesy Beef Enchiladas

Servings: 4
Cooking Time:xx
Ingredients:
- 500g minced beef
- 1 packet taco seasoning
- 8 tortillas
- 300g grated cheese
- 150g soured cream
- 1 can black beans
- 1 can chopped tomatoes
- 1 can mild chopped chillies
- 1 can red enchilada sauce
- 300g chopped coriander

Directions:
1. Brown the beef and add the taco seasoning
2. Add the beef, beans, tomatoes and chillies to the tortillas
3. Line the air fryer with foil and put the tortillas in
4. Pour the enchilada sauce over the top and sprinkle with cheese
5. Cook at 200°C for five minutes, remove from air fryer add toppings and serve

Pork Chops With Honey

Servings: 6
Cooking Time:xx
Ingredients:
- 2 ⅔ tbsp honey
- 100g ketchup
- 6 pork chops
- 2 cloves of garlic
- 2 slices mozzarella cheese

Directions:
1. Preheat air fryer to 200°C
2. Mix all the ingredients together in a bowl
3. Add the pork chops, allow to marinate for at least 1 hour
4. Place in the air fryer and cook for about 12 minutes turning halfway

Meatloaf

Servings: 2
Cooking Time:xx

Ingredients:
- 500g minced pork
- 1 egg
- 3 tbsp breadcrumbs
- 2 mushrooms thickly sliced
- 1 tbsp olive oil
- 1 chopped onion
- 1 tbsp chopped thyme
- 1 tsp salt
- Ground black pepper

Directions:
1. Preheat air fryer to 200°C
2. Combine all the ingredients in a bowl
3. Put the mix into a pan and press down firmly, coat with olive oil
4. Place pan in the air fryer and cook for 25 minutes

Parmesan Crusted Pork Chops

Servings: 6
Cooking Time:xx

Ingredients:
- 6 pork chops
- ½ tsp salt
- ¼ tsp pepper
- 1 tsp paprika
- 3 tbsp parmesan
- ½ tsp onion powder
- ¼ tsp chilli powder
- 2 eggs beaten
- 250g pork rind crumbs

Directions:
1. Preheat the air fryer to 200°C
2. Season the pork with the seasonings
3. Place the pork rind into a food processor and blend into crumbs
4. Mix the pork rind and seasonings in a bowl
5. Beat the eggs in a separate bowl
6. Dip the pork into the egg then into the crumb mix
7. Place pork in the air fryer and cook for about 15 minutes until crispy

Lamb Burgers

Servings: 4
Cooking Time:xx
Ingredients:
- 600g minced lamb
- 2 tsp garlic puree
- 1 tsp harissa paste
- 2 tbsp Moroccan spice
- Salt and pepper

Directions:
1. Place all the ingredients in a bowl and mix well
2. Form into patties
3. Place in the air fryer and cook at 180°C for 18 minutes

Tahini Beef Bites

Servings: 2
Cooking Time:xx
Ingredients:
- 500g sirloin steak, cut into cubes
- 2 tbsp Za'atar seasoning
- 1 tsp olive oil
- 25g Tahini
- 25g warm water
- 1 tbsp lemon juice
- 1 clove of garlic
- Salt to taste

Directions:
1. Preheat the air fryer to 250°C
2. Take a bowl and combine the oil with the steak, salt, and Za'atar seasoning
3. Place in the air fryer and cook for 10 minutes, turning halfway through
4. Take a bowl and combine the water, garlic, lemon juice, salt, and tahini, or use a food processor if you have one
5. Pour the sauce over the bites and serve

Tender Ham Steaks

Servings: 1
Cooking Time:xx
Ingredients:
- 1 ham steak
- 2 tbsp brown sugar
- 1 tsp honey
- 2 tbsp melted butter

Directions:
1. Preheat the air fryer to 220°C
2. Combine the melted butter and brown sugar until smooth
3. Add the ham to the air fryer and brush both sides with the butter mixture
4. Cook for 12 minutes, turning halfway through and re-brushing the ham
5. Drizzle honey on top before serving

Old Fashioned Steak

Servings: 4
Cooking Time:xx
Ingredients:
- 4 medium steaks
- 100g flour
- ½ tsp garlic powder
- Salt and pepper
- 1 egg
- 4 slices bacon
- 350ml milk

Directions:
1. Beat the egg
2. Mix the flour with garlic powder, salt and pepper
3. Dip the steak into the egg then cover in the flour mix
4. Place in the air fryer and cook at 170°C for 7 minutes, turnover and cook for another 10 minutes until golden brown
5. Whilst the steak is cooking, place the bacon in a frying pan, stir in the flour. Add milk to the bacon and stir until there are no lumps in the flour
6. Season with salt and pepper Cook for 2 minutes until thickened season with salt and pepper

Pulled Pork, Bacon, And Cheese Sliders

Servings:2
Cooking Time:30 Minutes
Ingredients:
- 2 x 50 g / 3.5 oz pork steaks
- 1 tsp salt
- 1 tsp black pepper
- 4 slices bacon strips, chopped into small pieces
- 1 tbsp soy sauce
- 1 tbsp BBQ sauce
- 100 g / 7 oz cheddar cheese, grated
- 2 bread buns

Directions:
1. Preheat the air fryer to 200 °C / 400 °F and line the bottom of the basket with parchment paper.
2. Place the pork steaks on a clean surface and season with salt and black pepper. Move the pork steak in the prepared air fryer basket and cook for 15 minutes.
3. Remove the steak from the air fryer and shred using two forks. Mix with the chopped bacon in a heatproof bowl and place the bowl in the air fryer. Cook for 10 minutes.
4. Remove the bowl from the air fryer and stir in the soy sauce and BBQ sauce. Return the bowl to the air fryer basket and continue cooking for a further 5 minutes.
5. Meanwhile, spread the cheese across one half of the bread buns. Top with the cooked pulled pork and an extra squirt of BBQ sauce.

Pork Taquitos

Servings: 5
Cooking Time:xx

Ingredients:
- 400g shredded pork
- 500g grated mozzarella
- 10 flour tortillas
- The juice of 1 lime
- Cooking spray

Directions:
1. Preheat air fryer to 190°C
2. Sprinkle lime juice on the pork and mix
3. Microwave tortilla for about 10 seconds to soften
4. Add a little pork and cheese to a tortilla
5. Roll then tortilla up, and place in the air fryer
6. Cook for about 7 minutes until golden, turn halfway through cooking

Chinese Pork With Pineapple

Servings: 4
Cooking Time:xx

Ingredients:
- 450g pork loin, cubed
- ½ tsp salt
- ½ tsp pepper
- 1 tbsp brown sugar
- 75g fresh coriander, chopped
- 2 tbsp toasted sesame seeds
- ½ pineapple, cubed
- 1 sliced red pepper
- 1 minced clove of garlic
- 1 tsp ginger
- 2 tbsp soy
- 1 tbsp oil

Directions:
1. Season the pork with salt and pepper
2. Add all ingredients to the air fryer
3. Cook at 180°C for 17 minutes
4. Serve and garnish with coriander and toasted sesame seeds

Fish & Seafood Recipes

Garlic-parsley Prawns

Servings: 2
Cooking Time:xx
Ingredients:
- 300 g/10½ oz. raw king prawns/jumbo shrimp (without shell)
- 40 g/3 tablespoons garlic butter, softened (see page 72)
- 2 tablespoons freshly chopped flat-leaf parsley

Directions:
1. Thread the prawns/shrimp onto 6 metal skewers that will fit your air-fryer. Mix together the softened garlic butter and parsley and brush evenly onto the prawn skewers.
2. Preheat the air-fryer to 180°C/350°F.
3. Place the skewers on an air-fryer liner or a piece of pierced parchment paper. Add the skewers to the preheated air-fryer and air-fry for 2 minutes, then turn the skewers over and cook for a further 2 minutes. Check the internal temperature of the prawns has reached at least 50°C/120°F using a meat thermometer – if not, cook for another few minutes and serve.

Shrimp Wrapped With Bacon

Servings: 2
Cooking Time:xx
Ingredients:
- 16 shrimp
- 16 slices of bacon
- 2 tbsp ranch dressing to serve

Directions:
1. Preheat the air fryer to 200°C
2. Wrap the shrimps in the bacon
3. Refrigerate for 30 minutes
4. Cook the shrimp for about 5 minutes turn them over and cook for a further 2 minutes
5. Serve with the ranch dressing on the side

Garlic Tilapia

Servings: 2
Cooking Time:xx
Ingredients:
- 2 tilapia fillets
- 2 tsp chopped fresh chives
- 2 tsp chopped fresh parsley
- 2 tsp olive oil
- 1 tsp minced garlic
- Salt and pepper for seasoning

Directions:
1. Preheat the air fryer to 220°C
2. Take a small bowl and combine the olive oil with the chives, garlic, parsley and a little salt and pepper
3. Brush the mixture over the fish fillets
4. Place the fish into the air fryer and cook for 10 minutes, until flaky

Traditional Fish And Chips

Servings: 4
Cooking Time:xx

Ingredients:
- 4 potatoes, peeled and cut into chips
- 2 fish fillets of your choice
- 1 beaten egg
- 3 slices of wholemeal bread, grated into breadcrumbs
- 25g tortilla crisps
- 1 lemon rind and juice
- 1 tbsp parsley
- Salt and pepper to taste

Directions:
1. Preheat your air fryer to 200ºC
2. Place the chips inside and cook until crispy
3. Cut the fish fillets into 4 slices and season with lemon juice
4. Place the breadcrumbs, lemon rind, parsley, tortillas and seasoning into a food processor and blitz to create a crumb consistency
5. Place the breadcrumbs on a large plate
6. Coat the fish in the egg and then the breadcrumb mixture
7. Cook for 15 minutes at 180ºC

Copycat Fish Fingers

Servings: 2
Cooking Time:xx

Ingredients:
- 2 slices wholemeal bread, grated into breadcrumbs
- 50g plain flour
- 1 beaten egg
- 1 white fish fillet
- The juice of 1 small lemon
- 1 tsp parsley
- 1 tsp thyme
- 1 tsp mixed herbs
- Salt and pepper to taste

Directions:
1. Preheat the air fryer to 180ºC
2. Add salt pepper and parsley to the breadcrumbs and combine well
3. Place the egg in another bowl
4. Place the flour in a separate bowl
5. Place the fish into a food processor and add the lemon juice, salt, pepper thyme and mixed herbs
6. Blitz to create a crumb-like consistency
7. Roll your fish in the flour, then the egg and then the breadcrumbs
8. Cook at 180ºC for 8 minutes

Tilapia Fillets

Servings: 2
Cooking Time:xx

Ingredients:
- 2 tbsp melted butter
- 150g almond flour
- 3 tbsp mayonnaise
- 2 tilapia fillets
- 25g thinly sliced almonds
- Salt and pepper to taste
- Vegetable oil spray

Directions:
1. Mix the almond flour, butter, pepper and salt together in a bowl
2. Spread mayonnaise on both sides of the fish
3. Cover the fillets in the almond flour mix
4. Spread one side of the fish with the sliced almonds
5. Spray the air fryer with the vegetable spray
6. Place in the air fryer and cook at 160°C for 10 minutes

Cajun Prawn Skewers

Servings: 2
Cooking Time:xx

Ingredients:
- 350 g/12 oz. king prawns/jumbo shrimp
- MARINADE
- 1 teaspoon smoked paprika
- 1 teaspoon unrefined sugar
- 1 teaspoon salt
- ½ teaspoon onion powder
- ½ teaspoon mustard powder
- ¼ teaspoon dried oregano
- ¼ teaspoon dried thyme
- 1 teaspoon white wine vinegar
- 2 teaspoons olive oil

Directions:
1. Mix all the marinade ingredients together in a bowl. Mix the prawns/shrimp into the marinade and cover. Place in the fridge to marinate for at least an hour.
2. Preheat the air-fryer to 180°C/350°F.
3. Thread 4–5 prawns/shrimp on to each skewer (you should have enough for 4–5 skewers). Add the skewers to the preheated air-fryer and air-fry for 2 minutes, then turn the skewers and cook for a further 2 minutes. Check the internal temperature of the prawns/shrimp has reached at least 50°C/125°F using a meat thermometer – if not, cook for another few minutes. Serve immediately.

Thai Salmon Patties

Servings: 7
Cooking Time:xx

Ingredients:
- 1 large can of salmon, drained and bones removed
- 30g panko breadcrumbs
- ¼ tsp salt
- 1 ½ tbsp Thai red curry paste
- 1 ½ tbsp brown sugar
- Zest of 1 lime
- 2 eggs
- Cooking spray

Directions:
1. Take a large bowl and combine all ingredients together until smooth
2. Use your hands to create patties that are around 1 inch in thickness
3. Preheat your air fryer to 180°C
4. Coat the patties with cooking spray
5. Cook for 4 minutes each side

Cod In Parma Ham

Servings: 2
Cooking Time:xx

Ingredients:
- 2 x 175–190-g/6–7-oz. cod fillets, skin removed
- 6 slices Parma ham or prosciutto
- 16 cherry tomatoes
- 60 g/2 oz. rocket/arugula
- DRESSING
- 1 tablespoon olive oil
- 1½ teaspoons balsamic vinegar
- garlic salt, to taste
- freshly ground black pepper, to taste

Directions:
1. Preheat the air-fryer to 180°C/350°F.
2. Wrap each piece of cod snugly in 3 ham slices. Add the ham-wrapped cod fillets and the tomatoes to the preheated air-fryer and air-fry for 6 minutes, turning the cod halfway through cooking. Check the internal temperature of the fish has reached at least 60°C/140°F using a meat thermometer – if not, cook for another minute.
3. Meanwhile, make the dressing by combining all the ingredients in a jar and shaking well.
4. Serve the cod and tomatoes on a bed of rocket/arugula with the dressing poured over.

Ranch Style Fish Fillets

Servings: 4
Cooking Time:xx

Ingredients:
- 200g bread crumbs
- 30g ranch-style dressing mix
- 2 tbsp oil
- 2 beaten eggs
- 4 fish fillets of your choice
- Lemon wedges to garnish

Directions:
1. Preheat air fryer to 180°C
2. Mix the bread crumbs and ranch dressing mix together, add in the oil until the mix becomes crumbly
3. Dip the fish into the, then cover in the breadcrumb mix
4. Place in the air fryer and cook for 12-13 minutes

Garlic Butter Salmon

Servings: 2
Cooking Time:xx

Ingredients:
- 2 salmon fillets, boneless with the skin left on
- 1 tsp minced garlic
- 2 tbsp melted butter
- 1 tsp chopped parsley
- Salt and pepper to taste

Directions:
1. Preheat the air fryer to 270 °C
2. Take a bowl and combine the melted butter, parsley and garlic to create a sauce
3. Season the salmon to your liking
4. Brush the salmon with the garlic mixture, on both sides
5. Place the salmon into the fryer, with the skin side facing down
6. Cook for 10 minutes - the salmon is done when it flakes with ease

Extra Crispy Popcorn Shrimp

Servings: 2
Cooking Time:xx

Ingredients:
- 300g Frozen popcorn shrimp
- 1 tsp cayenne pepper
- Salt and pepper for seasoning

Directions:
1. Preheat the air fryer to 220°C
2. Place the shrimp inside the air fryer and cook for 6 minutes, giving them a shake at the halfway point
3. Remove and season with salt and pepper, and the cayenne to your liking

Coconut Shrimp

Servings: 4
Cooking Time:xx

Ingredients:
- 250g flour
- 1 ½ tsp black pepper
- 2 eggs
- 150g unsweetened flaked coconut
- 1 Serrano chilli, thinly sliced
- 25g panko bread crumbs
- 300g shrimp raw
- ½ tsp salt
- 4 tbsp honey
- 25ml lime juice

Directions:
1. Mix together flour and pepper, in another bowl beat the eggs and in another bowl mix the panko and coconut
2. Dip each of the shrimp in the flour mix then the egg and then cover in the coconut mix
3. Coat the shrimp in cooking spray
4. Place in the air fryer and cook at 200°C for 6-8 mins turning half way through
5. Mix together the honey, lime juice and chilli and serve with the shrimp

Fish In Parchment Paper

Servings: 2
Cooking Time:xx

Ingredients:
- 250g cod fillets
- 1 chopped carrot
- 1 chopped fennel
- 1 tbsp oil
- 1 thinly sliced red pepper
- ½ tsp tarragon
- 1 tbsp lemon juice
- 1 tbsp salt
- ½ tsp ground pepper

Directions:
1. In a bowl, mix the tarragon and ½ tsp salt add the vegetables and mix well
2. Cut two large squares of parchment paper
3. Spray the cod with oil and cover both sides with salt and pepper
4. Place the cod in the parchment paper and add the vegetables
5. Fold over the paper to hold the fish and vegetables
6. Place in the air fryer and cook at 170°C for 15 minutes

Fish Sticks With Tartar Sauce Batter

Servings: 4
Cooking Time:xx
Ingredients:
- 6 tbsp mayonnaise
- 2 tbsp dill pickle
- 1 tsp seafood seasoning
- 400g cod fillets, cut into sticks
- 300g panko breadcrumbs

Directions:
1. Combine the mayonnaise, seafood seasoning and dill pickle in a large bowl.
2. Add the cod sticks and coat well
3. Preheat air fryer to 200°C
4. Coat the fish sticks in the breadcrumbs
5. Place in the air fryer and cook for 12 minutes

Oat & Parmesan Crusted Fish Fillets

Servings: 2
Cooking Time:xx
Ingredients:
- 20 g/⅓ cup fresh breadcrumbs
- 25 g/3 tablespoons oats
- 15 g/¼ cup grated Parmesan
- 1 egg
- 2 x 175-g/6-oz. white fish fillets, skin-on
- salt and freshly ground black pepper

Directions:
1. Preheat the air-fryer to 180°C/350°F.
2. Combine the breadcrumbs, oats and cheese in a bowl and stir in a pinch of salt and pepper. In another bowl beat the egg. Dip the fish fillets in the egg, then top with the oat mixture.
3. Add the fish fillets to the preheated air-fryer on an air-fryer liner or a piece of pierced parchment paper. Air-fry for 10 minutes. Check the fish is just flaking away when a fork is inserted, then serve immediately.

Salmon Patties

Servings: 4
Cooking Time:xx
Ingredients:
- 400g salmon
- 1 egg
- 1 diced onion
- 200g breadcrumbs
- 1 tsp dill weed

Directions:
1. Remove all bones and skin from the salmon
2. Mix egg, onion, dill weed and bread crumbs with the salmon
3. Shape mixture into patties and place into the air fryer
4. Set air fryer to 180°C
5. Cook for 5 minutes then turn them over and cook for a further 5 minutes until golden brown

Air Fried Scallops

Servings: 2
Cooking Time:xx
Ingredients:
- 6 scallops
- 1 tbsp olive oil
- Salt and pepper to taste

Directions:
1. Brush the filets with olive oil
2. Sprinkle with salt and pepper
3. Place in the air fryer and cook at 200°C for 2 mins
4. Turn the scallops over and cook for another 2 minutes

Store-cupboard Fishcakes

Servings: 3
Cooking Time:xx
Ingredients:
- 400 g/14 oz. cooked potato – either mashed potato or the insides of jacket potatoes (see page 124)
- 2 x 150–200-g/5½–7-oz. cans fish, such as tuna or salmon, drained
- 2 eggs
- ¾ teaspoon salt
- 1 teaspoon dried parsley
- ½ teaspoon freshly ground black pepper
- 1 tablespoon olive oil
- caper dressing (see page 79), to serve

Directions:
1. Mix the cooked potato, fish, eggs, salt, parsley and pepper together in a bowl, then divide into 6 equal portions and form into fishcakes. Drizzle the olive oil over both sides of each fishcake.
2. Preheat the air-fryer to 180°C/350°F.
3. Add the fishcakes to the preheated air-fryer and air-fry for 15 minutes, turning halfway through cooking. Serve with salad and tartare sauce or Caper Dressing.

Honey Sriracha Salmon

Servings: 2
Cooking Time:xx
Ingredients:
- 25g sriracha
- 25g honey
- 500g salmon fillets
- 1 tbsp soy sauce

Directions:
1. Mix the honey, soy sauce and sriracha, keep half the mix to one side for dipping
2. Place the salmon in the sauce skin side up and marinade for 30 minutes
3. Spray air fryer basket with cooking spray
4. Heat the air fryer to 200°C
5. Place salmon in the air fryer skin side down and cook for 12 minutes

Chilli Lime Tilapia

Servings: 3
Cooking Time:xx

Ingredients:
- 500g Tilapia fillets
- 25g panko crumbs
- 200g flour
- Salt and pepper to taste
- 2 eggs
- 1 tbsp chilli powder
- The juice of 1 lime

Directions:
1. Mix panko, salt and pepper and chilli powder together
2. Whisk the egg in a separate bowl
3. Spray the air fryer with cooking spray
4. Dip the tilapia in the flour, then in the egg and cover in the panko mix
5. Place fish in the air fryer, spray with cooking spray and cook for 7-8 minutes at 190°C
6. Turn the fish over and cook for a further 7-8 minutes until golden brown.
7. Squeeze lime juice over the top and serve

Mahi Fish Tacos

Servings: 4
Cooking Time:xx

Ingredients:
- 400g fresh mahi
- 8 small corn tortillas
- 2 tsp cajun seasoning
- 5 tbsp sour cream
- 2 tbsp mayonnaise
- 2 tbsp scotch bonnet pepper sauce (use 1 tbsp if you don't like your food too spicy)
- 1 tbsp sriracha sauce
- 2 tbsp lime juice
- Salt and pepper to taste
- 1 tbsp vegetable oil

Directions:
1. Clean the mahi. Cut into half inch slices and season with salt
2. Mix quarter parts cayenne pepper and black pepper with cajun seasoning. Sprinkle onto fish
3. Brush pepper sauce on both sides of the fish
4. Set the air fryer to 180°C and cook for about 10 minutes or until golden brown
5. Whilst the fish cooks make the chipotle lime cream. Mix the mayo, sour cream, lime juice sriracha and cayenne pepper
6. Assemble tacos and enjoy

Cajun Shrimp Boil

Servings: 6
Cooking Time:xx

Ingredients:
- 300g cooked shrimp
- 14 slices of smoked sausage
- 5 par boiled potatoes, cut into halves
- 4 mini corn on the cobs, quartered
- 1 diced onion
- 3 tbsp old bay seasoning
- Olive oil spray

Directions:
1. Combine all the ingredients in a bowl and mix well
2. Line the air fryer with foil
3. Place half the mix into the air fryer and cook at 200°C for about 6 minutes, mix the ingredients and cook for a further 6 minutes.
4. Repeat for the second batch

Cod Nuggets

Servings: 4
Cooking Time:xx

Ingredients:
- 400g cod fillets, cut into 8 chunks
- 35g flour
- 1 tbsp vegetable oil
- 200g cornflakes or cracker crumbs
- Egg wash - 1 tbsp egg and 1 tbsp water
- Salt and pepper to taste

Directions:
1. Crush the crackers or cornflakes to make crumbs, mix in the vegetable oil
2. Season the cod with salt and pepper and cover in flour, dip into the egg-wash then cover in crumbs
3. Set the air fryer to 180°C
4. Place the cod nuggets in the air fryer basket and cook for 15 minutes, until golden brown.

Poultry Recipes

Turkey And Mushroom Burgers

Servings: 2
Cooking Time:xx

Ingredients:
- 180g mushrooms
- 500g minced turkey
- 1 tbsp of your favourite chicken seasoning, e.g. Maggi
- 1 tsp onion powder
- 1 tsp garlic powder
- Salt and pepper to taste

Directions:
1. Place the mushrooms in a food processor and puree
2. Add all the seasonings and mix well
3. Remove from the food processor and transfer to a mixing bowl
4. Add the minced turkey and combine again
5. Shape the mix into 5 burger patties
6. Spray with cooking spray and place in the air fryer
7. Cook at 160°C for 10 minutes, until cooked.

Hawaiian Chicken

Servings: 2
Cooking Time:xx

Ingredients:
- 2 chicken breasts
- 1 tbsp butter
- A pinch of salt and pepper
- 160ml pineapple juice
- 25g brown sugar
- 3 tbsp soy sauce
- 2 tsp water
- 1 clove of garlic, minced
- 1 tsp grated ginger
- 2 tsp cornstarch

Directions:
1. Preheat the air fryer to 260°C
2. Take a bowl and combine the butter and salt and pepper
3. Cover the chicken with the butter and cook in the fryer for 15 minutes, turning halfway
4. Remove and allow to rest for 5 minutes
5. Take another bowl and mix together the pineapple juice, soy sauce, garlic, ginger, and brown sugar
6. Transfer to a saucepan and simmer for 5 minutes
7. Combine the water and cornstarch and add to the sauce, stirring continually for another minute
8. Slice the chicken into strips and pour the sauce over the top

Crunchy Chicken Tenders

Servings: 4
Cooking Time:xx

Ingredients:
- 8 regular chicken tenders (frozen work best)
- 1 egg
- 2 tbsp olive oil
- 150g dried breadcrumbs

Directions:
1. Heat the fryer to 175°C
2. In a small bowl, beat the egg
3. In another bowl, combine the oil and the breadcrumbs together
4. Take one tender and first dip it into the egg, and then cover it in the breadcrumb mixture
5. Place the tender into the fryer basket
6. Repeat with the rest of the tenders, arranging them carefully so they don't touch inside the basket
7. Cook for 12 minutes, checking that they are white in the centre before serving

Nashville Chicken

Servings: 4
Cooking Time:xx

Ingredients:
- 400g boneless chicken breast tenders
- 2 tsp salt
- 2 tsp coarsely ground black pepper
- 2 tbsp hot sauce
- 2 tbsp pickle juice
- 500g all purpose flour
- 3 large eggs
- 300ml buttermilk
- 2 tbsp olive oil
- 6 tbsp cayenne pepper
- 3 tbsp dark brown sugar
- 1 tsp chilli powder
- 1 tsp garlic powder
- 1 tsp paprika
- Salt and pepper to taste

Directions:
1. Take a large mixing bowl and add the chicken, hot sauce, pickle juice, salt and pepper and combine
2. Place in the refrigerator for 3 hours
3. Transfer the flour to a bowl
4. Take another bowl and add the eggs, buttermilk and 1 tbsp of the hot sauce, combining well
5. Press each piece of chicken into the flour and coat well
6. Place the chicken into the buttermilk mixture and then back into the flour
7. Allow to sit or 10 minutes
8. Preheat the air fryer to 193C
9. Whisk together the spices, brown sugar and olive oil to make the sauce and pour over the chicken tenders
10. Serve whilst still warm

Chicken Jalfrezi

Servings: 4
Cooking Time:xx
Ingredients:
- 500g chicken breasts
- 1 tbsp water
- 4 tbsp tomato sauce
- 1 chopped onion
- 1 chopped bell pepper
- 2 tsp love oil
- 1 tsp turmeric
- 1 tsp cayenne pepper
- 2 tsp garam masala
- Salt and pepper to taste

Directions:
1. Take a large mixing bowl and add the chicken, onions, pepper, salt, garam masala, turmeric, oil and cayenne pepper, combining well
2. Place the chicken mix in the air fryer and cook at 180ºC for 15 minutes
3. Take a microwave-safe bowl and add the tomato sauce, water salt, garam masala and cayenne, combining well
4. Cook in the microwave for 1 minute, stir then cook for a further minute
5. Remove the chicken from the air fryer and pour the sauce over the top.
6. Serve whilst still warm

Healthy Bang Bang Chicken

Servings: 4
Cooking Time:xx
Ingredients:
- 500g chicken breasts, cut into pieces of around 1" in size
- 1 beaten egg
- 50ml milk
- 1 tbsp hot pepper sauce
- 80g flour
- 70g tapioca starch
- 1 ½ tsp seasoned starch
- 1 tsp garlic granules
- ½ tsp cumin
- 6 tbsp plain Greek yogurt
- 3 tbsp sweet chilli sauce
- 1 tsp hot sauce

Directions:
1. Preheat the air fryer to 190ºC
2. Take a mixing bowl and combine the egg, milk and hot sauce
3. Take another bowl and combine the flour, tapioca starch, salt, garlic and cumin
4. Dip the chicken pieces into the sauce bowl and then into the flour bowl
5. Place the chicken into the air fryer
6. Whilst cooking, mix together the Greek yogurt, sweet chilli sauce and hot sauce and serve with the chicken

Chicken Parmesan With Marinara Sauce

Servings: 4
Cooking Time:xx

Ingredients:

- 400g chicken breasts, sliced in half
- 250g panko breadcrumbs
- 140g grated parmesan cheese
- 140g grated mozzarella cheese
- 3 egg whites
- 200g marinara sauce
- 2 tsp Italian seasoning
- Salt and pepper to taste
- Cooking spray

Directions:

1. Preheat the air fryer to 200°C
2. Lay the chicken slices on the work surface and pound with a mallet or a rolling pin to flatten
3. Take a mixing bowl and add the panko breadcrumbs, cheese and the seasoning, combining well
4. Add the egg whites into a separate bowl
5. Dip the chicken into the egg whites and then the breadcrumbs
6. Cook for 7 minutes in the air fryer

Satay Chicken Skewers

Servings: 4
Cooking Time:xx

Ingredients:

- 3 chicken breasts, chopped into 3 x 3-cm/1¼ x 1¼-in. cubes
- MARINADE
- 200 ml/¾ cup canned coconut milk (including the thick part from the can)
- 1 plump garlic clove, finely chopped
- 2 teaspoons freshly grated ginger
- 2 tablespoons soy sauce
- 1 heaped tablespoon peanut butter
- 1 tablespoon maple syrup
- 1 tablespoon mild curry powder
- 1 tablespoon fish sauce

Directions:

1. Mix the marinade ingredients thoroughly in a bowl, then toss in the chopped chicken and stir to coat thoroughly. Leave in the fridge to marinate for at least 4 hours.
2. Preheat the air-fryer to 190°C/375°F.
3. Thread the chicken onto 8 metal skewers. Add to the preheated air-fryer (you may need to cook these in two batches, depending on the size of your air-fryer). Air-fry for 10 minutes. Check the internal temperature of the chicken has reached at least 74°C/165°F using a meat thermometer – if not, cook for another few minutes and then serve.

Chicken Fried Rice

Servings: 4
Cooking Time:xx
Ingredients:
- 400g cooked white rice
- 400g cooked chicken, diced
- 200g frozen peas and carrots
- 6 tbsp soy sauce
- 1 tbsp vegetable oil
- 1 diced onion

Directions:
1. Take a large bowl and add the rice, vegetable oil and soy sauce and combine well
2. Add the frozen peas, carrots, diced onion and the chicken and mix together well
3. Pour the mixture into a nonstick pan
4. Place the pan into the air fryer
5. Cook at 182C for 20 minutes

Chicken Tikka Masala

Servings: 4
Cooking Time:xx
Ingredients:
- 100g tikka masala curry pasta
- 200g low fat yogurt
- 600g skinless chicken breasts
- 1 tbsp vegetable oil
- 1 onion, chopped
- 400g can of the whole, peeled tomatoes
- 20ml water
- 1 tbsp sugar
- 2 tbsp lemon juice
- 1 small bunch of chopped coriander leaves

Directions:
1. Take a bowl and combine the tikka masala curry paste with half the yogurt
2. Cut the chicken into strips
3. Preheat the air fryer to 200°C
4. Add the yogurt mixture and coat the chicken until fully covered
5. Place into the refrigerator for 2 hours
6. Place the oil and onion in the air fryer and cook for 10 minutes
7. Add the marinated chicken, tomatoes, water and the rest of the yogurt and combine
8. Add the sugar and lemon juice and combine again
9. Cook for 15 minutes

Olive Stained Turkey Breast

Servings: 14
Cooking Time:xx

Ingredients:
- The brine from a can of olives
- 150ml buttermilk
- 300g boneless and skinless turkey breasts
- 1 sprig fresh rosemary
- 2 sprigs fresh thyme

Directions:
1. Take a mixing bowl and combine the olive brine and buttermilk
2. Pour the mixture over the turkey breast
3. Add the rosemary and thyme sprigs
4. Place into the refrigerator for 8 hours
5. Remove from the fridge and let the turkey reach room temperature
6. Preheat the air fryer to 175C
7. Cook for 15 minutes, ensuring the turkey is cooked through before serving

Air Fried Maple Chicken Thighs

Servings: 4
Cooking Time:xx

Ingredients:
- 200ml buttermilk
- ½ tbsp maple syrup
- 1 egg
- 1 tsp granulated garlic salt
- 4 chicken thighs with the bone in
- 140g all purpose flour
- 65g tapioca flour
- 1 tsp sweet paprika
- 1 tsp onion powder
- ¼ tsp ground black pepper
- ¼ tsp cayenne pepper
- ½ tsp granulated garlic
- ½ tsp honey powder

Directions:
1. Take a bowl and combine the buttermilk, maple syrup, egg and garlic powder
2. Transfer to a bag and add chicken thighs, shaking to combine well
3. Set aside for 1 hour
4. Take a shallow bowl and add the flour, tapioca flour, salt, sweet paprika, smoked paprika, pepper, cayenne pepper and honey powder, combining well
5. Preheat the air fryer to 190°C
6. Drag the chicken through flour mixture and place the chicken skin side down in the air fryer Cook for 12 minutes, until white in the middle

Pizza Chicken Nuggets

Servings: 2
Cooking Time:xx

Ingredients:
- 60 g/¾ cup dried breadcrumbs (see page 9)
- 20 g/¼ cup grated Parmesan
- ½ teaspoon dried oregano
- ¼ teaspoon freshly ground black pepper
- 150 g/⅔ cup Mediterranean sauce (see page 102) or 150 g/5½ oz. jarred tomato pasta sauce (keep any leftover sauce for serving)
- 400 g/14 oz. chicken fillets

Directions:
1. Preheat the air-fryer to 180°C/350°F.
2. Combine the breadcrumbs, Parmesan, oregano and pepper in a bowl. Have the Mediterranean or pasta sauce in a separate bowl.
3. Dip each chicken fillet in the tomato sauce first, then roll in the breadcrumb mix until coated fully.
4. Add the breaded fillets to the preheated air-fryer and air-fry for 10 minutes. Check the internal temperature of the chicken has reached at least 74°C/165°F using a meat thermometer – if not, cook for another few minutes.
5. Serve with some additional sauce that has been warmed through.

Honey Cajun Chicken Thighs

Servings: 6
Cooking Time:xx

Ingredients:
- 100ml buttermilk
- 1 tsp hot sauce
- 400g skinless, boneless chicken thighs
- 150g all purpose flour
- 60g tapioca flour
- 2.5 tsp cajun seasoning
- ½ tsp garlic salt
- ½ tsp honey powder
- ¼ tsp ground paprika
- ⅛ tsp cayenne pepper
- 4 tsp honey

Directions:
1. Take a large bowl and combine the buttermilk and hot sauce
2. Transfer to a plastic bag and add the chicken thighs
3. Allow to marinate for 30 minutes
4. Take another bowl and add the flour, tapioca flour, cajun seasoning, garlic, salt, honey powder, paprika, and cayenne pepper, combining well
5. Dredge the chicken through the mixture
6. Preheat the air fryer to 175C
7. Cook for 15 minutes before flipping the thighs over and cooking for another 10 minutes
8. Drizzle 1 tsp of honey over each thigh

Chicken & Potatoes

Servings: 4
Cooking Time:xx
Ingredients:
- 2 tbsp olive oil
- 2 potatoes, cut into 2" pieces
- 2 chicken breasts, cut into pieces of around 1" size
- 4 crushed garlic cloves
- 2 tsp smoked paprika
- 1 tsp thyme
- 1/2 tsp red chilli flakes
- Salt and pepper to taste

Directions:
1. Preheat your air fryer to 260°C
2. Take a large bowl and combine the potatoes with half of the garlic, half the paprika, half the chilli flakes, salt, pepper and half the oil
3. Place into the air fryer and cook for 5 minutes, before turning over and cooking for another 5 minutes
4. Take a bowl and add the chicken with the rest of the seasonings and oil, until totally coated
5. Add the chicken to the potatoes mixture, moving the potatoes to the side
6. Cook for 10 minutes, turning the chicken halfway through

Bacon Wrapped Chicken Thighs

Servings: 4
Cooking Time:xx
Ingredients:
- 75g softened butter
- ½ clove minced garlic
- ¼ tsp dried thyme
- ¼ tsp dried basil
- ⅛ tsp coarse salt
- 100g thick cut bacon
- 350g chicken thighs, boneless and skinless
- 2 tsp minced garlic
- Salt and pepper to taste

Directions:
1. Take a mixing bowl and add the softened butter, garlic, thyme, basil, salt and pepper, combining well
2. Place the butter onto a sheet of plastic wrap and roll up to make a butter log
3. Refrigerate for about 2 hours
4. Remove the plastic wrap
5. Place one bacon strip onto the butter and then place the chicken thighs on top of the bacon. Sprinkle with garlic
6. Place the cold butter into the middle of the chicken thigh and tuck one end of bacon into the chicken
7. Next, fold over the chicken thigh whilst rolling the bacon around
8. Repeat with the rest
9. Preheat the air fryer to 188C
10. Cook the chicken until white in the centre and the juices run clear

Charred Chicken Breasts

Servings: 2
Cooking Time:xx

Ingredients:
- 2 tsp paprika
- 1 tsp ground thyme
- 1 tsp cumin
- ½ tsp cayenne pepper
- ½ tsp onion powder
- ½ tsp black pepper
- ¼ tsp salt
- 2 tsp vegetable oil
- 2 skinless boneless chicken breasts, cut into halves

Directions:
1. Take a bowl and add the paprika, thyme, cumin, cayenne pepper, onion powder, black pepper and salt
2. Coat each chicken breast with oil and dredge chicken in the spice mixture
3. Preheat air fryer to 175C
4. Cook for 10 minutes and flip
5. Cook for 10 more minutes

Chicken Fajitas

Servings: 3
Cooking Time:xx

Ingredients:
- 2 boneless chicken breasts, sliced into strips
- 5 mini (bell) peppers, sliced into strips
- 1 courgette/zucchini, sliced into 5-mm/¼-in. thick discs
- 2 tablespoons olive oil
- 28-g/1-oz. packet fajita seasoning mix
- TO SERVE
- wraps
- sliced avocado
- chopped tomato and red onion
- grated Red Leicester cheese
- plain yogurt
- coriander/cilantro
- lime wedges, for squeezing

Directions:
1. Combine the chicken, (bell) peppers, courgettes/zucchini and olive oil in a bowl. Add the fajita seasoning and stir to coat.
2. Preheat the air-fryer to 180°C/350°F.
3. Add the coated vegetables and chicken to the preheated air-fryer and air-fry for 12 minutes, shaking the drawer a couple of times during cooking. Check the internal temperature of the chicken has reached at least 74°C/165°F using a meat thermometer – if not, cook for another few minutes.
4. Serve immediately alongside the serving suggestions or your own choices of accompaniments.

Grain-free Chicken Katsu

Servings: 4
Cooking Time:xx

Ingredients:

- 125 g/1¼ cups ground almonds
- ½ teaspoon salt
- ½ teaspoon garlic powder
- ½ teaspoon dried parsley
- ½ teaspoon freshly ground black pepper
- ¼ teaspoon onion powder
- ¼ teaspoon dried oregano
- 450 g/1 lb. mini chicken fillets
- 1 egg, beaten
- oil, for spraying/drizzling
- coriander/cilantro leaves, to serve
- KATSU SAUCE
- 1 teaspoon olive oil or avocado oil
- 1 courgette/zucchini (approx. 150 g/5 oz.), finely chopped
- 1 carrot (approx. 100 g/3½ oz.), finely chopped
- 1 onion (approx. 120 g/4½ oz.), finely chopped
- 1 eating apple (approx. 150 g/5 oz.), cored and finely chopped
- 1 teaspoon ground ginger
- 1 teaspoon ground turmeric
- 2 teaspoons ground cumin
- 2 teaspoons ground coriander
- 1½ teaspoons mild chilli/chili powder
- 1 teaspoon garlic powder
- 1½ tablespoons runny honey
- 1 tablespoon soy sauce (gluten-free if you wish)
- 700 ml/3 cups vegetable stock (700 ml/3 cups water with 1½ stock cubes)

Directions:

1. First make the sauce. The easiest way to ensure all the vegetables and apple are finely chopped is to combine them in a food processor. Heat the oil in a large saucepan and sauté the finely chopped vegetables and apple for 5 minutes. Add all the seasonings, honey, soy sauce and stock and stir well, then bring to a simmer and simmer for 30 minutes.
2. Meanwhile, mix together the ground almonds, seasonings and spices. Dip each chicken fillet into the beaten egg, then into the almond-spice mix, making sure each fillet is fully coated. Spray the coated chicken fillets with olive oil (or simply drizzle over).
3. Preheat the air-fryer to 180°C/350°F.
4. Place the chicken fillets in the preheated air-fryer and air-fry for 10 minutes, turning halfway through cooking. Check the internal temperature of the chicken has reached at least 74°C/165°F using a meat thermometer – if not, cook for another few minutes.
5. Blend the cooked sauce in a food processor until smooth. Serve the chicken with the Katsu Sauce drizzled over (if necessary, reheat the sauce gently before serving) and scattered with coriander leaves. Any unused sauce can be frozen.

Whole Chicken

Servings: 4
Cooking Time:xx
Ingredients:
- 1.5-kg/3¼-lb. chicken
- 2 tablespoons butter or coconut oil
- salt and freshly ground black pepper

Directions:
1. Place the chicken breast-side up and carefully insert the butter or oil between the skin and the flesh of each breast. Season.
2. Preheat the air-fryer to 180°C/350°F. If the chicken hits the heating element, remove the drawer to lower the chicken a level.
3. Add the chicken to the preheated air-fryer breast-side up. Air-fry for 30 minutes, then turn over and cook for a further 10 minutes. Check the internal temperature with a meat thermometer. If it is 75°C/167°F at the thickest part, remove the chicken from the air-fryer and leave to rest for 10 minutes before carving. If less than 75°C/167°F, continue to cook until this internal temperature is reached and then allow to rest.

Chicken And Cheese Chimichangas

Servings: 6
Cooking Time:xx
Ingredients:
- 100g shredded chicken (cooked)
- 150g nacho cheese
- 1 chopped jalapeño pepper
- 6 flour tortillas
- 5 tbsp salsa
- 60g refried beans
- 1 tsp cumin
- 0.5 tsp chill powder
- Salt and pepper to taste

Directions:
1. Take a large mixing bowl and add all of the ingredients, combining well
2. Add ⅓ of the filling to each tortilla and roll into a burrito shape
3. Spray the air fryer with cooking spray and heat to 200°C
4. Place the chimichangas in the air fryer and cook for 7 minutes

Buffalo Chicken Wontons

Servings: 6
Cooking Time:xx
Ingredients:
- 200g shredded chicken
- 1 tbsp buffalo sauce
- 4 tbsp softened cream cheese
- 1 sliced spring onion
- 2 tbsp blue cheese crumbles
- 12 wonton wrappers

Directions:
1. Preheat the air fryer to 200°C
2. Take a bowl and combine the chicken and buffalo sauce
3. In another bowl mix the cream cheese until a smooth consistency has formed and then combine the scallion blue cheese and seasoned chicken
4. Take the wonton wrappers and run wet fingers along each edge
5. Place 1 tbsp of the filling into the centre of the wonton and fold the corners together
6. Cook at 200°C for 3 to 5 minutes, until golden brown

Pepper & Lemon Chicken Wings

Servings: 2
Cooking Time:xx
Ingredients:
- 1kg chicken wings
- 1/4 tsp cayenne pepper
- 2 tsp lemon pepper seasoning
- 3 tbsp butter
- 1 tsp honey
- An extra 1 tsp lemon pepper seasoning for the sauce

Directions:
1. Preheat the air fryer to 260°C
2. Place the lemon pepper seasoning and cayenne in a bowl and combine
3. Coat the chicken in the seasoning
4. Place the chicken in the air fryer and cook for 20 minutes, turning over halfway
5. Turn the temperature up to 300°C and cook for another 6 minutes
6. Meanwhile, melt the butter and combine with the honey and the rest of the seasoning
7. Remove the wings from the air fryer and pour the sauce over the top

Side Dishes Recipes

Aubergine Parmesan

Servings: 4
Cooking Time:xx
Ingredients:
- 100g Italian breadcrumbs
- 50g grated parmesan
- 1 tsp Italian seasoning
- 1 tsp salt
- ½ tsp dried basil
- ½ tsp onion powder
- ½ tsp black pepper
- 100g flour
- 2 eggs
- 1 aubergine, sliced into ½ inch rounds

Directions:
1. Mix breadcrumbs, parmesan, salt Italian seasoning, basil, onion powder and pepper in a bowl
2. Add the flour to another bowl, and beat the eggs in another
3. Dip the aubergine in the flour, then the eggs and then coat in the bread crumbs
4. Preheat the air fryer to 185°C
5. Place the aubergine in the air fryer and cook for 8-10 minutes
6. Turnover and cook for a further 4-6 minutes

Hasselback New Potatoes

Servings: 4
Cooking Time:xx
Ingredients:
- 8–12 new potatoes, roughly 5–7 cm/2–2¾ in. in length
- 2 teaspoons olive oil
- salt
- 1 tablespoon butter (optional)

Directions:
1. Preheat the air-fryer to 180°C/350°F.
2. Slice the potatoes multiple times widthways, making sure you do not cut all the way through (if you place the potatoes in the bowl of a wooden spoon to make these slices, it prevents you cutting all the way through). Coat the potatoes in the olive oil and sprinkle over the salt.
3. Add the potatoes to the preheated air-fryer and air-fry for 20–25 minutes until the potatoes are crispy on the outside but soft on the inside. Serve immediately.

Butternut Squash Fries

Servings: 4
Cooking Time:xx
Ingredients:
- 400g butternut squash, cut into sticks
- 1 tbsp olive oil
- 2 tbsp bagel seasoning
- 1 tsp fresh chopped rosemary

Directions:
1. Preheat air fryer to 200°C
2. Drizzle butternut squash with olive oil mix to coat
3. Add to the air fryer, cook for about 22 minutes until golden brown, stirring every 4 minutes
4. Sprinkle with bagel seasoning to serve

Sweet Potato Tots

Servings: 24
Cooking Time:xx
Ingredients:
- 2 sweet potatoes, peeled
- ½ tsp cajun seasoning
- Olive oil cooking spray
- Sea salt to taste

Directions:
1. Boil the sweet potatoes in a pan for about 15 minutes, allow to cool
2. Grate the sweet potato and mix in the cajun seasoning
3. Form into tot shaped cylinders
4. Spray the air fryer with oil, place the tots in the air fryer
5. Sprinkle with salt and cook for 8 minutes at 200°C, turn and cook for another 8 minutes

Onion Rings

Servings: 4
Cooking Time:xx

Ingredients:
- 200g flour
- 75g cornstarch
- 2 tsp baking powder
- 1 tsp salt
- 2 pinches of paprika
- 1 large onion, cut into rings
- 1 egg
- 1 cup milk
- 200g breadcrumbs
- 2 pinches garlic powder

Directions:
1. Stir flour, salt, starch and baking powder together in a bowl
2. Dip onion rings into the flour mix to coat
3. Whisk the egg and milk into the flour mix, dip in the onion rings
4. Dip the onion rings into the bread crumbs
5. Heat the air fryer to 200°C
6. Place the onion rings in the air fryer and cook for 2-3 minutes until golden brown
7. Sprinkle with paprika and garlic powder to serve

Stuffed Jacket Potatoes

Servings: 4
Cooking Time:xx

Ingredients:
- 2 large russet potatoes
- 2 tsp olive oil
- 100ml yoghurt
- 100ml milk
- ¼ tsp pepper
- 50g chopped spinach
- 2 tbsp nutritional yeast
- ½ tsp salt

Directions:
1. Preheat the air fryer to 190°C
2. Rub the potatoes with oil
3. Place the potatoes in the air fryer and cook for 30 minutes, turn and cook for a further 30 minutes
4. Cut each potato in half and scoop out the middles, mash with yoghurt, milk and yeast. Stir in the spinach and season with salt and pepper
5. Add the mix back into the potato skins and place in the air fryer, cook at 160°C for about 5 mins

Ranch-style Potatoes

Servings: 2
Cooking Time:xx

Ingredients:
- 300g baby potatoes, washed
- 1 tbsp olive oil
- 3 tbsp dry ranch seasoning

Directions:
1. Preheat the air fryer to 220°C
2. Cut the potatoes in half
3. Take a mixing bowl and combine the olive oil with the ranch seasoning
4. Add the potatoes to the bowl and toss to coat
5. Cook for 15 minutes, shaking halfway through

Asparagus Fries

Servings: 2
Cooking Time:xx

Ingredients:
- 1 egg
- 1 tsp honey
- 100g panko bread crumbs
- Pinch of cayenne pepper
- 100g grated parmesan
- 12 asparagus spears
- 75g mustard
- 75g Greek yogurt

Directions:
1. Preheat air fryer to 200°C
2. Combine egg and honey in a bowl, mix panko crumbs and parmesan on a plate
3. Coat each asparagus in egg then in the bread crumbs
4. Place in the air fryer and cook for about 6 mins
5. Mix the remaining ingredients in a bowl and serve as a dipping sauce

Pumpkin Fries

Servings: 4
Cooking Time:xx

Ingredients:
- 1 small pumpkin, seeds removed and peeled, cut into half inch slices
- 2 tsp olive oil
- 1 tsp garlic powder
- 1/2 tsp paprika
- A pinch of salt

Directions:
1. Take a large bowl and add the slices of pumpkin
2. Add the oil and all the seasonings. Toss to coat well
3. Place in the air fryer
4. Cook at 280°C for 15 minutes, until the chips are tender, shaking at the halfway point

Bbq Beetroot Crisps

Servings: 4
Cooking Time: 5 Minutes
Ingredients:
- 400 g / 14 oz beetroot, sliced
- 2 tbsp olive oil
- 1 tbsp BBQ seasoning
- ½ tsp black pepper

Directions:
1. Preheat the air fryer to 180 °C / 350 °F and line the bottom of the basket with parchment paper.
2. Place the beetroot slices in a large bowl. Add the olive oil, BBQ seasoning, and black pepper, and toss to coat the beetroot slices on both sides.
3. Place the beetroot slices in the air fryer and cook for 5 minutes until hot and crispy.

Orange Sesame Cauliflower

Servings: 4
Cooking Time: xx
Ingredients:
- 100ml water
- 30g cornstarch
- 50g flour
- 1/2 tsp salt
- ½ tsp pepper
- 2 tbsp tomato ketchup
- 2 tbsp brown sugar
- 1 sliced onion

Directions:
1. Mix together flour, cornstarch, water, salt and pepper until smooth
2. Coat the cauliflower and chill for 30 minutes
3. Place in the air fryer and cook for 22 minutes at 170°C
4. Meanwhile combine remaining ingredients in a saucepan, gently simmer until thickened.
5. Mix cauliflower with sauce and top with toasted sesame seeds to serve

Cheesy Garlic Asparagus

Servings: 4
Cooking Time: xx
Ingredients:
- 1 tsp olive oil
- 500g asparagus
- 1 tsp garlic salt
- 1 tbsp grated parmesan cheese
- Salt and pepper for seasoning

Directions:
1. Preheat the air fryer to 270°C
2. Clean the asparagus and cut off the bottom 1"
3. Pat dry and place in the air fryer, covering with the oil
4. Sprinkle the parmesan and garlic salt on top, seasoning to your liking
5. Cook for between 7 and 10 minutes
6. Add a little extra parmesan over the top before serving

Crispy Broccoli

Servings: 2
Cooking Time:xx
Ingredients:
- 170 g/6 oz. broccoli florets
- 2 tablespoons olive oil
- ⅛ teaspoon garlic salt
- ⅛ teaspoon freshly ground black pepper
- 2 tablespoons freshly grated Parmesan or Pecorino

Directions:
1. Preheat the air-fryer to 200°C/400°F.
2. Toss the broccoli in the oil, season with the garlic salt and pepper, then toss over the grated cheese and combine well. Add the broccoli to the preheated air-fryer and air-fry for 5 minutes, giving the broccoli a stir halfway through to ensure even cooking.

Grilled Bacon And Cheese

Servings: 2
Cooking Time:xx
Ingredients:
- 4 slices of regular bread
- 1 tbsp butter
- 2 slices cheddar cheese
- 5 slices bacon, pre-cooked
- 2 slices mozzarella cheese

Directions:
1. Place the butter into the microwave to melt
2. Spread the butter onto one side of the bread slices
3. Place one slice of bread into the fryer basket, with the buttered side facing downwards
4. Place the cheddar on top, followed by the bacon, mozzarella and the other slice of bread, with the buttered side facing upwards
5. Set your fryer to 170°C and cook the sandwich for 4 minutes
6. Turn the sandwich over and cook for another 3 minutes
7. Turn the sandwich out and serve whilst hot
8. Repeat with the other remaining sandwich

Asparagus Spears

Servings: 2
Cooking Time:xx
Ingredients:
- 1 bunch of trimmed asparagus
- 1 teaspoon olive oil
- ¼ teaspoon salt
- ⅛ teaspoon freshly ground black pepper

Directions:
1. Preheat the air-fryer to 180°C/350°F.
2. Toss the asparagus spears in the oil and seasoning. Add these to the preheated air-fryer and air-fry for 8–12 minutes, turning once (cooking time depends on the thickness of the stalks, which should retain some bite).

Butternut Squash

Servings: 4
Cooking Time:xx
Ingredients:
- 500 g/1 lb. 2 oz. butternut squash, chopped into 2.5-cm/1-in. cubes
- 1 tablespoon olive oil or avocado oil
- 1 teaspoon smoked paprika
- 1 teaspoon dried oregano
- ½ teaspoon salt
- ¼ teaspoon freshly ground black pepper

Directions:
1. Preheat the air-fryer to 180°C/350°F.
2. In a bowl toss the butternut squash cubes in the oil and all the seasonings.
3. Add the butternut squash cubes to the preheated air-fryer and air-fry for 16–18 minutes, shaking the drawer once during cooking.

Honey Roasted Parsnips

Servings: 4
Cooking Time:xx
Ingredients:
- 350 g/12 oz. parsnips
- 1 tablespoon plain/all-purpose flour (gluten-free if you wish)
- 1½ tablespoons runny honey
- 2 tablespoons olive oil
- salt

Directions:
1. Top and tail the parsnips, then slice lengthways, about 2 cm/¾ in. wide. Place in a saucepan with water to cover and a good pinch of salt. Bring to the boil, then boil for 5 minutes.
2. Remove and drain well, allowing any excess water to evaporate. Dust the parsnips with flour. Mix together the honey and oil in a small bowl, then toss in the parsnips to coat well in the honey and oil.
3. Preheat the air-fryer to 180°C/350°F.
4. Add the parsnips to the preheated air-fryer and air-fry for 14–16 minutes, depending on how dark you like the outsides (the longer you cook them, the sweeter they get).

Super Easy Fries

Servings: 2
Cooking Time:xx
Ingredients:
- 500g potatoes cut into ½ inch sticks
- 1 tsp olive oil
- ¼ tsp salt
- ¼ tsp pepper

Directions:
1. Place the potatoes in a bowl cover with water and allow to soak for 30 minutes
2. Spread the butter onto one side of the bread slices
3. Pat dry with paper, drizzle with oil and toss to coat
4. Place in the air fryer and cook at 200°C for about 15 minutes, keep tossing through cooking time
5. Sprinkle with salt and pepper

Celery Root Fries
Servings: 2
Cooking Time:xx
Ingredients:
- ½ celeriac, cut into sticks
- 500ml water
- 1 tbsp lime juice
- 1 tbsp olive oil
- 75g mayo
- 1 tbsp mustard
- 1 tbsp powdered horseradish

Directions:
1. Put celeriac in a bowl, add water and lime juice, soak for 30 minutes
2. Preheat air fryer to 200
3. Mix together the mayo, horseradish powder and mustard, refrigerate
4. Drain the celeriac, drizzle with oil and season with salt and pepper
5. Place in the air fryer and cook for about 10 minutes turning halfway
6. Serve with the mayo mix as a dip

Shishito Peppers
Servings: 2
Cooking Time:xx
Ingredients:
- 200g shishito peppers
- Salt and pepper to taste
- ½ tbsp avocado oil
- 75g grated cheese
- 2 limes

Directions:
1. Rinse the peppers
2. Place in a bowl and mix with oil, salt and pepper
3. Place in the air fryer and cook at 175°C for 10 minutes
4. Place on a serving plate and sprinkle with cheese

Corn On The Cob
Servings: 4
Cooking Time:xx
Ingredients:
- 75g mayo
- 2 tsp grated cheese
- 1 tsp lime juice
- ¼ tsp chilli powder
- 2 ears of corn, cut into 4

Directions:
1. Heat the air fryer to 200°C
2. Mix the mayo, cheese lime juice and chilli powder in a bowl
3. Cover the corn in the mayo mix
4. Place in the air fryer and cook for 8 minutes

Sweet Potato Wedges

Servings:4
Cooking Time:20 Minutes
Ingredients:
- ½ tsp garlic powder
- ½ tsp cumin
- ½ tsp smoked paprika
- ½ tsp cayenne pepper
- ½ tsp salt
- ½ tsp black pepper
- 1 tsp dried chives
- 4 tbsp olive oil
- 3 large sweet potatoes, cut into wedges

Directions:
1. Preheat the air fryer to 180 °C / 350 °F and line the bottom of the basket with parchment paper.
2. In a bowl, mix the garlic powder, cumin, smoked paprika, cayenne pepper, salt, black pepper, and dried chives until combined.
3. Whisk in the olive oil and coat the sweet potato wedges in the spicy oil mixture.
4. Transfer the coated sweet potatoes to the air fryer and close the lid. Cook for 20 minutes until cooked and crispy. Serve hot as a side with your main meal.

Yorkshire Puddings

Servings: 2
Cooking Time:xx
Ingredients:
- 1 tablespoon olive oil
- 70 g/½ cup plus ½ tablespoon plain/all-purpose flour (gluten-free if you wish)
- 100 ml/7 tablespoons milk
- 2 eggs
- salt and freshly ground black pepper

Directions:
1. You will need 4 ramekins. Preheat the air-fryer to 200°C/400°F.
2. Using a pastry brush, oil the base and sides of each ramekin, dividing the oil equally between the ramekins. Place the greased ramekins in the preheated air-fryer and heat for 5 minutes.
3. Meanwhile, in a food processor or using a whisk, combine the flour, milk, eggs and seasoning until you have a batter that is frothy on top. Divide the batter equally between the preheated ramekins. Return the ramekins to the air-fryer and air-fry for 20 minutes without opening the drawer. Remove the Yorkshire puddings from the ramekins and serve immediately.

Desserts Recipes

Pumpkin Spiced Bread Pudding

Servings: 2
Cooking Time:xx

Ingredients:
- 175g heavy cream
- 500g pumpkin puree
- 30ml milk
- 25g sugar
- 1 large egg, plus one extra yolk
- ⅛ tsp salt
- ½ tsp pumpkin spice
- 500g cubed crusty bread
- 4 tbsp butter

Directions:
1. Place all of the ingredients apart from the bread and butter into a bowl and mix.
2. Add the bread and melted butter to the bowl and mix well
3. Heat the air fryer to 175°C
4. Pour the mix into a baking tin and cook in the air fryer for 35-40 minutes
5. Serve with maple cream

Profiteroles

Servings: 9
Cooking Time:xx

Ingredients:
- 100g butter
- 200g plain flour
- 6 eggs
- 300ml water
- 2 tsp vanilla extract
- 300ml whipped cream
- 100g milk chocolate
- 2 tbsp whipped cream
- 50g butter
- 2 tsp icing sugar

Directions:
1. Preheat the air fryer to 170°C
2. Place the butter and water in a pan over a medium heat, bring to the boil, remove from the heat and stir in the flour
3. Return to the heat stirring until a dough is formed
4. Mix in the eggs and stir until mixture is smooth, make into profiterole shapes and cook in the air fryer for 10 minutes
5. For the filling whisk together 300ml whipped cream, vanilla extract and the icing sugar
6. For the topping place the butter, 2tbsp whipped cream and chocolate in a bowl and melt over a pan of hot water until mixed together
7. Pipe the filling into the roles and finish off with a chocolate topping

Lemon Pies
Servings: 6
Cooking Time:xx
Ingredients:
- 1 pack of pastry
- 1 egg beaten
- 200g lemon curd
- 225g powdered sugar
- ½ lemon

Directions:
1. Preheat the air fryer to 180°C
2. Cut out 6 circles from the pastry using a cookie cutter
3. Add 1 tbsp of lemon curd to each circle, brush the edges with egg and fold over
4. Press around the edges of the dough with a fork to seal
5. Brush the pies with the egg and cook in the air fryer for 10 minutes
6. Mix the lemon juice with the powdered sugar to make the icing and drizzle on the cooked pies

Cinnamon-maple Pineapple Kebabs
Servings: 2
Cooking Time:xx
Ingredients:
- 4 x pineapple strips, roughly 2 x 2 cm/¾ x ¾ in. by length of pineapple
- 1 teaspoon maple syrup
- ½ teaspoon vanilla extract
- ¼ teaspoon ground cinnamon
- Greek or plant-based yogurt and grated lime zest, to serve

Directions:
1. Line the air-fryer with an air-fryer liner or a piece of pierced parchment paper. Preheat the air-fryer to 180°C/350°F.
2. Stick small metal skewers through the pineapple lengthways. Mix the maple syrup and vanilla extract together, then drizzle over the pineapple and sprinkle over the cinnamon.
3. Add the skewers to the preheated lined air-fryer and air-fry for 15 minutes, turning once. If there is any maple-vanilla mixture left after the initial drizzle, then drizzle this over the pineapple during cooking too. Serve with yogurt and lime zest.

Cherry Pies
Servings: 6
Cooking Time:xx
Ingredients:
- 300g prepared shortcrust pastry
- 75g cherry pie filling
- Cooking spray
- 3 tbsp icing sugar
- ½ tsp milk

Directions:
1. Cut out 6 pies with a cookie cutter
2. Add 1 ½ tbsp filling to each pie
3. Fold the dough in half and seal around the edges with a fork
4. Place in the air fryer, spray with cooking spray
5. Cook at 175°C for 10 minutes
6. Mix icing sugar and milk and drizzled over cooled pies to serve

Fruit Scones

Servings: 4
Cooking Time:xx
Ingredients:
- 225g self raising flour
- 50g butter
- 50g sultanas
- 25g caster sugar
- 1 egg
- A little milk

Directions:
1. Place the flour in a bowl and rub in the butter, add the sultanas and mix
2. Stir in the caster sugar
3. Add the egg and mix well
4. Add a little bit of milk at a time to form a dough
5. Shape the dough into scones
6. Place in the air fryer and bake at 180°C for 8 minutes

Cinnamon Bites

Servings: 8
Cooking Time:xx
Ingredients:
- 200g flour
- 200g whole wheat flour
- 2 tbsp sugar
- 1 tsp baking powder
- ¼ tsp cinnamon
- 3 tbsp water
- ¼ tsp salt
- 4 tbsp butter
- 25ml milk
- Cooking spray
- 350g powdered sugar

Directions:
1. Mix together flour, sugar, baking powder and salt in a bowl
2. Add the butter and mix well
3. Add the milk and mix to form a dough
4. Knead until dough is smooth, cut into 16 pieces
5. Roll each piece into a small ball
6. Coat the air fryer with cooking spray and heat to 175°C
7. Add the balls to the air fryer and cook for 12 minutes
8. Mix the powdered sugar and water together, decorate

Pop Tarts

Servings: 6
Cooking Time:xx

Ingredients:

- 200g strawberries quartered
- 25g sugar
- ½ pack ready made pie crust
- Cooking spray
- 50g powdered sugar
- 1 ½ tsp lemon juice
- 1 tbsp sprinkles

Directions:

1. Stir together strawberries and sugar in a bowl
2. Allow to stand for 15 minutes then microwave on high for 10 minutes stirring halfway through
3. Roll out pie crust into 12 inch circle, cut into 12 rectangles
4. Spoon mix onto 6 of the rectangles
5. Brush the edges with water and top with the remaining rectangles
6. Press around the edges with a fork to seal
7. Place in the air fryer and cook at 175°C for about 10 minutes
8. Mix together powdered sugar and decorate add sprinkles

Granola Bars

Servings: 6
Cooking Time:xx

Ingredients:

- 250g oats
- 60g melted butter
- 30g sugar
- 3 tbsp honey
- Handful of raisins
- 1 apple cooked and peeled
- 1 tbsp olive oil
- 1 tsp vanilla
- 1 tsp cinnamon

Directions:

1. Add all the dry ingredients to the blender and mix
2. Add all the wet ingredients to the air fryer pan and mix well
3. Add the dry ingredients and mix well
4. Add the raisins and press down the mix into the pan
5. Cook for 10 mins at 160°C then at 5 minutes for 180°C
6. Chop into bars and serve

Sweet Potato Dessert Fries

Servings: 4
Cooking Time:xx
Ingredients:
- 2 sweet potatoes, peeled
- ½ tbsp coconut
- 1 tbsp arrowroot
- 2 tsp melted butter
- ½ cup coconut sugar
- 2 tsp cinnamon
- Icing sugar

Directions:
1. Cut the potatoes into ½ inch thick strips, coat in arrowroot and coconut oil
2. Place in the air fryer and cook at 190°C for 18 minutes shaking halfway through
3. Remove from air fryer and place in a bowl, drizzle with melted butter
4. Mix in sugar and cinnamon
5. Sprinkle with icing sugar to serve

Chocolate Eclairs

Servings: 9
Cooking Time:xx
Ingredients:
- 100g plain flour
- 50g butter
- 3 eggs
- 150ml water
- 25g butter
- 1 tsp vanilla extract
- 1 tsp icing sugar
- 150ml whipped cream
- 50g milk chocolate
- 1 tbsp whipped cream

Directions:
1. Preheat the air fryer to 180°C
2. Add 50g of butter to a pan along with the water and melt over a medium heat
3. Remove from the heat and stir in the flour. Return to the heat until mix form a single ball of dough
4. Allow to cool, once cool beat in the eggs until you have a smooth dough
5. Make into eclair shapes, cook in the air fryer at 180°C for 10 minutes and then 160°C for 8 minutes
6. Mix the vanilla, icing sugar and 150ml of whipping cream until nice and thick
7. Once cool fill each eclair with the cream mix
8. Place the chocolate, 1 tbsp whipped cream and 25g of butter in a glass bowl and melt over a pan of boiling water. Top the eclairs

Blueberry Muffins

Servings: 12
Cooking Time:xx
Ingredients:
- 500g cups self raising flour
- 50g monk fruit
- 50g cream
- 225g oil
- 2 eggs
- 200g blueberries
- Zest and juice of 1 lemon
- 1 tbsp vanilla

Directions:
1. Mix together flour and sugar, set aside
2. In another bowl mix the remaining ingredients
3. Mix in the flour
4. Spoon the mix into silicone cupcake cases
5. Place in the air fryer and cook at 160°C for about 10 minutes

Banana Maple Flapjack

Servings:9
Cooking Time:xx
Ingredients:
- 100 g/7 tablespoons butter (or plant-based spread if you wish)
- 75 g/5 tablespoons maple syrup
- 2 ripe bananas, mashed well with the back of a fork
- 1 teaspoon vanilla extract
- 240 g/2½ cups rolled oats/quick-cooking oats

Directions:
1. Gently heat the butter and maple syrup in a medium saucepan over a low heat until melted. Stir in the mashed banana, vanilla and oats and combine all ingredients. Pour the flapjack mixture into a 15 x 15-cm/6 x 6-in. baking pan and cover with foil.
2. Preheat the air-fryer to 200°C/400°F.
3. Add the baking pan to the preheated air-fryer and air-fry for 12 minutes, then remove the foil and cook for a further 4 minutes to brown the top. Leave to cool before cutting into 9 squares.

Oat-covered Banana Fritters

Servings: 4
Cooking Time:xx
Ingredients:
- 3 tablespoons plain/all-purpose flour (gluten-free if you wish)
- 1 egg, beaten
- 90 g/3 oz. oatcakes (gluten-free if you wish) or oat-based cookies, crushed to a crumb consistency
- 1½ teaspoons ground cinnamon
- 1 tablespoon unrefined sugar
- 4 bananas, peeled

Directions:
1. Preheat the air-fryer to 180°C/350°F.
2. Set up three bowls – one with flour, one with beaten egg and the other with the oatcake crumb, cinnamon and sugar mixed together. Coat the bananas in flour, then in egg, then in the crumb mixture.
3. Add the bananas to the preheated air-fryer and air-fry for 10 minutes. Serve warm.

Zebra Cake

Servings: 6
Cooking Time:xx

Ingredients:
- 115g butter
- 2 eggs
- 100g caster sugar
- 1 tbsp cocoa powder
- 100g self raising flour
- 30ml milk
- 1tsp vanilla

Directions:
1. Preheat air fryer to 160°C
2. Line a 6 inch baking tin
3. Beat together the butter and sugar until light and fluffy
4. Add eggs one at a time then add the vanilla and milk
5. Add the flour and mix well
6. Divide the mix in half
7. Add cocoa powder to half the mix and mix well
8. Add a scoop of each of the batters at a time until it's all in the tin, place in the air fryer and cook for 30 minutes

Banana Cake

Servings: 4
Cooking Time:xx

Ingredients:
- Cooking spray
- 25g brown sugar
- ½ tbsp butter
- 1 banana, mashed
- 1 egg
- 2 tbsp honey
- 225g self raising flour
- ½ tsp cinnamon
- Pinch salt

Directions:
1. Preheat air fryer to 160°C
2. Spray a small fluted tube tray with cooking spray
3. Beat sugar and butter together in a bowl until creamy
4. Combine the banana egg and honey together in another bowl
5. Mix into the butter until smooth
6. Sift in the remaining ingredients and mix well
7. Spoon into the tray and cook in the air fryer for 30 minutes

Butter Cake

Servings: 4
Cooking Time:xx
Ingredients:
- Cooking spray
- 7 tbsp butter
- 25g white sugar
- 2 tbsp white sugar
- 1 egg
- 300g flour
- Pinch salt
- 6 tbsp milk

Directions:
1. Preheat air fryer to 175°C
2. Spray a small fluted tube pan with cooking spray
3. Beat the butter and all of the sugar together in a bowl until creamy
4. Add the egg and mix until fluffy, add the salt and flour mix well. Add the milk and mix well
5. Put the mix in the pan and cook in the air fryer for 15 minutes

Birthday Cheesecake

Servings: 8
Cooking Time:xx
Ingredients:
- 6 Digestive biscuits
- 50g melted butter
- 800g soft cheese
- 500g caster sugar
- 4 tbsp cocoa powder
- 6 eggs
- 2 tbsp honey
- 1 tbsp vanilla

Directions:
1. Flour a spring form tin to prevent sticking
2. Crush the biscuits and then mix with the melted butter, press into the bottom and sides of the tin
3. Mix the caster sugar and soft cheese with an electric mixer. Add 5 eggs, honey and vanilla. Mix well
4. Spoon half the mix into the pan and pat down well. Place in the air fryer and cook at 180°C for 20 minutes then 160°C for 15 minutes and then 150°C for 20 minutes
5. Mix the cocoa and the last egg into the remaining mix. Spoon over the over the bottom layer and place in the fridge. Chill for 11 hours

S'mores

Servings: 2
Cooking Time:xx
Ingredients:
- 2 graham crackers, broken in half
- 2 marshmallows, halved
- 2 pieces of chocolate

Directions:
1. Place 2 halves of graham crackers in the air fryer and add a marshmallow to each sticky side down
2. Cook in the air fryer at 180°C for 5 minutes until the marshmallows are golden
3. Remove from the air fryer add a piece of chocolate and top with the other half of graham crackers

Chocolate Orange Muffins

Servings: 12
Cooking Time:xx
Ingredients:
- 100g self raising flour
- 110g caster sugar
- 50g butter
- 20g cocoa powder
- 50ml milk
- 1 tsp cocoa nibs
- 1 large orange juice and rind
- 1 tbsp honey
- 1tsp vanilla essence
- 2 eggs

Directions:
1. Add the flour, butter and sugar to a mixing bowl and rug together
2. Add the cocoa, honey, orange and vanilla mix well
3. Mix the milk and egg together then add to the flour mix, combine well
4. Rub your muffin cases with flour to stop them sticking, add 2 tbsp batter to each one
5. Cook in the air fryer for 12 minutes at 180°C

Chocolate Soufflé

Servings: 2
Cooking Time:xx
Ingredients:
- 150g semi sweet chocolate, chopped
- ¼ cup butter
- 2 eggs, separated
- 3 tbsp sugar
- ½ tsp vanilla extract
- 2 tbsp flour
- Icing sugar
- Whipped cream to serve

Directions:
1. Butter and sugar 2 small ramekins
2. Melt the chocolate and butter together
3. In another bowl beat the egg yolks, add the sugar and vanilla beat well
4. Drizzle in the chocolate mix well, add the flour and mix well
5. Preheat the air fryer to 165°C
6. Whisk the egg whites to soft peaks, gently fold into the chocolate mix a little at a time
7. Add the mix to ramekins and place in the air fryer. Cook for about 14 minutes
8. Dust with icing sugar, serve with whipped cream

Pecan & Molasses Flapjack

Servings:9
Cooking Time:xx

Ingredients:
- 120 g/½ cup plus 2 teaspoons butter or plant-based spread, plus extra for greasing
- 40 g/2 tablespoons blackstrap molasses
- 60 g/5 tablespoons unrefined sugar
- 50 g/½ cup chopped pecans
- 200 g/1½ cups porridge oats/steelcut oats (not rolled or jumbo)

Directions:
1. Preheat the air-fryer to 180°C/350°F.
2. Grease and line a 15 x 15-cm/6 x 6-in. baking pan.
3. In a large saucepan melt the butter/spread, molasses and sugar. Once melted, stir in the pecans, then the oats. As soon as they are combined, tip the mixture into the prepared baking pan and cover with foil.
4. Place the foil-covered baking pan in the preheated air-fryer and air-fry for 10 minutes. Remove the foil, then cook for a further 2 minutes to brown the top. Leave to cool, then cut into 9 squares.

Apple And Cinnamon Empanadas

Servings: 12
Cooking Time:xx

Ingredients:
- 12 empanada wraps
- 2 diced apples
- 2 tbsp honey
- 1 tsp vanilla extract
- 1 tsp cinnamon
- ⅛ tsp nutmeg
- Olive oil spray
- 2 tsp cornstarch
- 1 tsp water

Directions:
1. Place apples, cinnamon, honey, vanilla and nutmeg in a pan cook for 2-3 minutes until apples are soft
2. Mix the cornstarch and water add to the pan and cook for 30 seconds
3. Add the apple mix to each of the empanada wraps
4. Roll the wrap in half, pinch along the edges, fold the edges in then continue to roll to seal
5. Place in the air fryer and cook at 200°C for 8 minutes, turn and cook for another 10 minutes

Spiced Apples

Servings: 4
Cooking Time:xx

Ingredients:
- 4 apples, sliced
- 2 tbsp ghee
- 2 tbsp sugar
- 1 tsp apple pie spice

Directions:
1. Place apples in a bowl, add the ghee and sprinkle with sugar and apple pie spice
2. Place in a tin that will fit the air fryer
3. Heat the air fryer to 175°C
4. Put the tin in the air fryer and cook for 10 minutes until tender

Chocolate And Berry Pop Tarts

Servings: 8
Cooking Time: 10 Minutes
Ingredients:
- For the filling:
- 50 g / 1.8 oz fresh raspberries
- 50 g / 1.8 oz fresh strawberries
- 100 g / 3.5 oz granulated sugar
- 1 tsp corn starch
- For the pastry:
- 1 sheet puff pastry
- For the frosting:
- 4 tbsp powdered sugar
- 2 tbsp maple syrup or honey
- Chocolate sprinkles

Directions:
1. Preheat the air fryer to 180 °C / 350 °F and line the mesh basket with parchment paper or grease it with olive oil.
2. Make the filling by combining the strawberries, raspberries, and granulated sugar in a saucepan. Place on medium heat until the mixture starts to boil. When it begins to boil, turn the temperature down to a low setting. Use a spoon to break up the berries and forms a smooth mixture.
3. Stir in the corn starch and let the mixture simmer for 1-2 minutes. Remove the saucepan from the heat and set aside to cool while you prepare the pastry.
4. Roll out the large sheet of puff pastry and cut it into 8 equal rectangles.
5. Spoon 2 tbsp of the cooled berry filling onto one side of each rectangle. Fold over the other side of each puff pastry rectangle to cover the filling. Press the sides down with a fork or using your fingers to seal the filling into the pastry.
6. Transfer the puff pastry rectangles into the lined air fryer basket. Cook for 10-12 minutes until the pastry is golden and crispy.
7. Meanwhile, make the frosting. Whisk together the powdered sugar, maple syrup or honey, and chocolate chips in a bowl until well combined.
8. Carefully spread a thin layer of frosting in the centre of each pop tart. Allow the frosting to set before serving.

Chocolate Mug Cake

Servings: 1
Cooking Time: xx
Ingredients:
- 30g self raising flour
- 5 tbsp sugar
- 1 tbsp cocoa powder
- 3 tbsp milk
- 3 tsp coconut oil

Directions:
1. Mix all the ingredients together in a mug
2. Heat the air fryer to 200°C
3. Place the mug in the air fryer and cook for 10 minutes

Christmas Biscuits

Servings: 8
Cooking Time:xx

Ingredients:
- 225g self raising flour
- 100g caster sugar
- 100g butter
- Juice and rind of orange
- 1 egg beaten
- 2 tbsp cocoa
- 2 tsp vanilla essence
- 8 pieces dark chocolate

Directions:
1. Preheat the air fryer to 180°C
2. Rub the butter into the flour. Add the sugar, vanilla, orange and cocoa mix well
3. Add the egg and mix to a dough
4. Split the dough into 8 equal pieces
5. Place a piece of chocolate in each piece of dough and form into a ball covering the chocolate
6. Place in the air fryer and cook for 15 minutes

Strawberry Lemonade Pop Tarts

Servings: 12
Cooking Time:xx

Ingredients:
- 300g whole wheat flour
- 225g white flour
- ¼ tsp salt
- 2 tbsp light brown sugar
- 300g icing sugar
- 2 tbsp lemon juice
- Zest of 1 lemon
- 150g cold coconut oil
- 1 tsp vanilla extract
- 75ml ice cold water
- Strawberry Jam
- 1 tsp melted coconut oil
- ¼ tsp vanilla extract
- Sprinkles

Directions:
1. In a bowl mix the flours, salt and sugar. Mix in the cold coconut oil
2. Add 1 tsp vanilla and 1 tbsp at a time of the ice cold water, mix until a dough is formed
3. Take the dough and roll out thinly on a floured surface. Cut into 5cm by 7cm rectangles
4. Place a tsp of jam in the centre of half the rectangles, wet the edges place another rectangle on the top and seal
5. Place in the air fryer and cook at 200°C for 10 minutes. Allow to cool
6. Mix the icing sugar, coconut oil, lemon juice and lemon zest in a bowl. Mix well. Top the pop tarts and add sprinkles to serve

Chocolate-glazed Banana Slices

Servings:2
Cooking Time:10 Minutes
Ingredients:
- 2 bananas
- 1 tbsp honey
- 1 tbsp chocolate spread, melted
- 2 tbsp milk chocolate chips

Directions:
1. Preheat the air fryer to 180 °C / 350 °F. Remove the mesh basket from the machine and line it with parchment paper.
2. Cut the two bananas into even slices and place them in the lined air fryer basket.
3. In a small bowl, mix the honey and melted chocolate spread. Use a brush to glaze the banana slices. Carefully press the milk chocolate chips into the banana slices enough so that they won't fall out when you transfer the bananas into the air fryer.
4. Carefully slide the mesh basket into the air fryer, close the lid, and cook for 10 minutes until the bananas are hot and the choc chips have melted.
5. Enjoy the banana slices on their own or with a side of ice cream.

Crispy Snack Apples

Servings: 2
Cooking Time:xx
Ingredients:
- 3 apples, Granny Smith work best
- 250g flour
- 3 whisked eggs
- 25g sugar
- 1 tsp ground cinnamon
- 250g cracker crumbs

Directions:
1. Preheat the air fryer to 220°C
2. Peel the apples, remove the cores and cut into wedges
3. Take three bowls - the first with the flour, the second with the egg, and then this with the cracker crumbs, sugar and cinnamon combined
4. Dip the apple wedges into the egg in order
5. Place in the air fryer and cook for 5 minutes, turning over with one minute remaining

Fruit Crumble

Servings: 2
Cooking Time:xx
Ingredients:
- 1 diced apple
- 75g frozen blackberries
- 25g brown rice flour
- 2 tbsp sugar
- ½ tsp cinnamon
- 2 tbsp butter

Directions:
1. Preheat air fryer to 150°C
2. Mix apple and blackberries in an air fryer safe baking pan
3. In a bowl mix the flour, sugar, cinnamon and butter, spoon over the fruit
4. Cook for 15 minutes

Pistachio Brownies

Servings: 4
Cooking Time:xx

Ingredients:
- 75ml milk
- ½ tsp vanilla extract
- 25g salt
- 25g pecans
- 75g flour
- 75g sugar
- 25g cocoa powder
- 1 tbsp ground flax seeds

Directions:
1. Mix all of the dry ingredients together, in another bowl mix the wet ingredients
2. Add all the ingredients together and mix well
3. Preheat the air fryer to 175°C
4. Line a 5 inch cake tin with parchment paper
5. Pour the brownie mix into the cake tin and cook in the air fryer for about 20 minutes

Grain-free Millionaire's Shortbread

Servings:9
Cooking Time:xx

Ingredients:
- BASE
- 60 g/5 tablespoons coconut oil
- 1 tablespoon maple syrup
- ½ teaspoon vanilla extract
- 180 g/1¾ cups ground almonds
- a pinch of salt
- MIDDLE
- 185 g/1⅓ cups dried pitted dates (soak in hot water for at least 20 minutes, then drain)
- 2 tablespoons almond butter
- 90 g/scant ½ cup canned coconut milk (the thick part once it has separated is ideal)
- TOPPING
- 125 g/½ cup coconut oil
- 4 tablespoons cacao powder
- 1 tablespoon maple syrup

Directions:
1. Preheat the air-fryer to 180°C/350°F.
2. To make the base, in a small saucepan melt the coconut oil with the maple syrup and vanilla extract. As soon as the coconut oil is melted, stir in the almonds and the salt off the heat. Press this mixture into a 15 x 15-cm/6 x 6-in. baking pan.
3. Add the baking pan to the preheated air-fryer and cook for 4 minutes, until golden brown on top. Remove from the air-fryer and allow to cool.
4. In a food processor, combine the rehydrated drained dates, almond butter and coconut milk. Once the base is cool, pour this mixture over the base and pop into the freezer to set for an hour.
5. After the base has had 45 minutes in the freezer, make the topping by heating the coconut oil in a saucepan until melted, then whisk in the cacao powder and maple syrup off the heat to make a chocolate syrup. Leave this to cool for 15 minutes, then pour over the set middle layer and return to the freezer for 30 minutes. Cut into 9 squares to serve.

RECIPES INDEX

A

Air Fried Maple Chicken Thighs 76
Air Fried Scallops 68
Air-fried Artichoke Hearts 39
Apple And Cinnamon Empanadas 100
Apple Crisps 12
Arancini 34
Artichoke Crostini 33
Artichoke Pasta 35
Asparagus Fries 85
Asparagus Spears 87
Aubergine Parmesan 82
Aubergine Parmigiana 32
Avocado Fries 14

B

Baba Ganoush 16
Bacon Wrapped Chicken Thighs 78
Bagel Pizza 34
Baked Feta, Tomato & Garlic Pasta 37
Banana Cake 97
Banana Maple Flapjack 96
Bbq Beetroot Crisps 86
Bbq Ribs 48
Bbq Soy Curls 38
Beef Bulgogi Burgers 49
Beef Nacho Pinwheels 51
Beef Stroganoff 54
Beef Stuffed Peppers 54
Beef Wellington 47
Beetroot Crisps 30
Birthday Cheesecake 98
Blueberry Bread 19
Blueberry Muffins 96
Bocconcini Balls 20
Breakfast Doughnuts 14
Breakfast Sausage Burgers 15
Buffalo Chicken Wontons 81
Butter Cake 98
Buttermilk Pork Chops 52
Butternut Squash 88
Butternut Squash Falafel 33
Butternut Squash Fries 83

C

Cajun Prawn Skewers 63
Cajun Shrimp Boil 70
Celery Root Fries 89
Char Siu Buffalo 46
Charred Chicken Breasts 79
Cheeseburger Egg Rolls 50
Cheesy Beef Enchiladas 56
Cheesy Garlic Asparagus 86
Cheesy Sausage Breakfast Pockets 12
Cherry Pies 92
Chicken & Potatoes 78
Chicken And Cheese Chimichangas 81
Chicken Fajitas 79
Chicken Fried Rice 75
Chicken Jalfrezi 73
Chicken Parmesan With Marinara Sauce 74
Chicken Tikka Masala 75
Chickpea And Sweetcorn Falafel 41
Chilli Lime Tilapia 69
Chinese Pork With Pineapple 60
Chocolate And Berry Pop Tarts 101

Chocolate Eclairs 95

Chocolate Mug Cake 101

Chocolate Orange Muffins 99

Chocolate Soufflé 99

Chocolate-glazed Banana Slices 103

Christmas Biscuits 102

Cinnamon Bites 93

Cinnamon-maple Pineapple Kebabs 92

Coconut Shrimp 66

Cod In Parma Ham 64

Cod Nuggets 70

Copycat Fish Fingers 62

Corn Nuts 22

Corn On The Cob 89

Courgette Fries 17

Courgette Meatballs 42

Crispy Broccoli 87

Crispy Chili Sausages 52

Crispy Potato Peels 35

Crispy Snack Apples 103

Crunchy Chicken Tenders 72

Crunchy Mexican Breakfast Wrap 18

E

Easy Air Fryer Sausage 19

Easy Cheese & Bacon Toasties 16

Easy Cheesy Scrambled Eggs 13

European Pancakes 19

Extra Crispy Popcorn Shrimp 65

F

Falafel Burgers 38

Fish In Parchment Paper 66

Fish Sticks With Tartar Sauce Batter 67

Focaccia Bread 28

French Toast 18

Fruit Crumble 103

Fruit Scones 93

G

Garlic Butter Salmon 65

Garlic Cheese Bread 22

Garlic Pizza Toast 24

Garlic Tilapia 61

Garlic-parsley Prawns 61

Grain-free Chicken Katsu 80

Grain-free Millionaire's Shortbread 104

Granola Bars 94

Grilled Bacon And Cheese 87

H

Halloumi Fries 20

Hasselback New Potatoes 83

Hawaiian Chicken 71

Healthy Bang Bang Chicken 73

Healthy Stuffed Peppers 13

Honey & Mustard Meatballs 56

Honey Cajun Chicken Thighs 77

Honey Roasted Parsnips 88

Honey Sriracha Salmon 68

I

Italian Rice Balls 24

J

Jalapeño Pockets 26

Japanese Pork Chops 46

K

Kheema Meatloaf 55

Korean Chicken Wings 28

L

Lamb Burgers 58

Lemon Pies 92

Lumpia 29

M

Mac & Cheese Bites 27

Mahi Fish Tacos 69

Meatloaf 57

Meaty Egg Cups 15

Mexican Breakfast Burritos 17

Mongolian Beef 47

Morning Sausage Wraps 15

Mozzarella Sticks 25

Muhammara 13

Mushroom Pasta 43

Mustard Pork Tenderloin 51

N

Nashville Chicken 72

O

Oat & Parmesan Crusted Fish Fillets 67

Oat-covered Banana Fritters 96

Old Fashioned Steak 59

Olive Stained Turkey Breast 76

Onion Rings 84

Orange Sesame Cauliflower 86

Orange Zingy Cauliflower 39

P

Parmesan Crusted Pork Chops 57

Pecan & Molasses Flapjack 100

Pepper & Lemon Chicken Wings 82

Pepperoni Bread 23

Peppers With Aioli Dip 22

Pistachio Brownies 104

Pizza Chicken Nuggets 77

Pop Tarts 94

Popcorn Tofu 21

Pork Chops With Honey 56

Pork Chops With Raspberry And Balsamic 53

Pork Jerky 21

Pork Taquitos 60

Potato Patties 23

Pretzel Bites 27

Profiteroles 91

Pulled Pork, Bacon, And Cheese Sliders 59

Pumpkin Fries 85

Pumpkin Spiced Bread Pudding 91

Q

Quinoa-stuffed Romano Peppers 32

R

Radish Hash Browns 40

Rainbow Vegetables 41

Ranch Style Fish Fillets 65

Ranch-style Potatoes 85

Raspberry Breakfast Pockets 20

Roast Beef 47

Roast Cauliflower & Broccoli 34

Roasted Almonds 29

Roasted Cauliflower 45

Roasted Vegetable Pasta 42

S

S'mores 98

Saganaki 30

Salmon Patties 67

Satay Chicken Skewers 74

Sausage Gnocchi One Pot 52

Shishito Peppers 89

Shrimp Wrapped With Bacon 61

Snack Style Falafel 26

Spanakopita Bites 44

Spiced Apples 100

Spicy Spanish Potatoes 35

Spinach And Feta Croissants 31

Spring Ratatouille 36

Steak Popcorn Bites 50

Sticky Asian Beef 53

Sticky Tofu With Cauliflower Rice 44

Store-cupboard Fishcakes 68

Strawberry Lemonade Pop Tarts 102

Stuffed Jacket Potatoes 84

Stuffed Peppers 40

Super Easy Fries 88

Sweet Potato Dessert Fries 95

Sweet Potato Taquitos 36

Sweet Potato Tots 83

Sweet Potato Wedges 90

T

Taco Lasagne Pie 55

Tahini Beef Bites 58

Tasty Pumpkin Seeds 30

Tempura Veggies 43

Tender Ham Steaks 58

Thai Bites 25

Thai Salmon Patties 64

Tilapia Fillets 63

Tofu Bowls 37

Traditional Empanadas 49

Traditional Fish And Chips 62

Turkey And Mushroom Burgers 71

Two-step Pizza 31

V

Vegetable & Beef Frittata 48

Veggie Bakes 40

Veggie Lasagne 45

W

Waffle Fries 29

Whole Chicken 81

Wholegrain Pitta Chips 14

Y

Yorkshire Puddings 90

Z

Zebra Cake 97

Printed in Great Britain
by Amazon